Prai

With this book, Rev. Dr. _____
pastor in our congregation, where it has been my privilege to serve with him as
assistant pastor for the last ten years. Like his sermons we are blessed to hear,
this book presents the deep truths of God's Holy Word in regard to His Holy
name in a manner that is profound yet practical, clear and engaging, challeng-
ing and comforting. May all who read this marvelous book continue to find
comfort and joy in the one true eternal God: Father, Son, and Holy Spirit!

REV. DR. MATTHEW C. HARRISON,
PRESIDENT, THE LUTHERAN CHURCH—MISSOURI SYNOD,
ASSISTANT PASTOR, VILLAGE LUTHERAN CHURCH, LADUE, MISSOURI

What is God's name? Why is the manner in which we speak His name so important that it is the Second Commandment? Isn't a name just a name? Rev.
Dr. Kevin Golden has produced a scholarly, concise, and accessible work on
the Lord's name that answers these questions and more. Indeed, perhaps the
greatest accomplishment of the book is that it draws attention to the importance and consequence of the Lord's name. The author directs the book to the
layperson theologian. As one of those, with limited theological training, nil
training in biblical languages, and yet a fervent desire to understand, I was genuinely pleased to be educated and even inspired by this book. The author di-
rectly attaches personal examples to biblical passages, making a difficult issue
easily relatable. The writing is masterfully engaging. Every word of this book
was obviously chosen with care and with the intent of enlightening readers. It
is a wonder to be educated so thoroughly about a topic that one was ignorant
of being ignorant of. This is a book worth consideration for Bible studies, for
children's education, for catechesis, and indeed, by any Christian. This book is
a gift worth reading again and again.

STEPHEN M. SAUNDERS, PHD,
PROFESSOR OF PSYCHOLOGY, MARQUETTE UNIVERSITY

This interesting, readable book, *Blessed Be His Name*, delivers a panoramic view
concerning the holiness of God's name that we Christians sometimes, in different ways, thoughtlessly and sinfully misuse. The book's many cogent points
remind us of God's Second Commandment, which we so easily forget both before and as we violate it. Christians reading this book will find it insightful and
spiritually beneficial.

ALVIN J. SCHMIDT, PHD,
PROFESSOR EMERITUS OF SOCIOLOGY, ILLINOIS COLLEGE,
AUTHOR OF *HOW CHRISTIANITY CHANGED THE WORLD* (2004)
AND *HALLMARKS OF LUTHERAN IDENTITY* (2017)

Kevin Golden has written a glowing book, and if there is just one recommendation I would make for the rising generation of young Christian readers, it would be to not only read but also absorb the profundity of this powerful, timely, and topical book. What's in a name? We hear this cliché from time to time, but if we apply it to the name above all names, God Almighty Himself, we come to see that we are standing on genuinely holy ground, all the while His sovereign presence is transforming, renewing, and changing our perception of all of life. Pastor Golden has evoked the blessedness of God in a new and nourishing way, and I am humbled by the power of his perceptions and learnedness.

TIMOTHY S. GOEGLEIN,
VICE PRESIDENT, FOCUS ON THE FAMILY, WASHINGTON, DC

In an age of conjecture, Rev. Golden's book brings a studied clarity to the subject of God's holy name. Each chapter, packed full of edifying goodness and truth from Scripture, offers golden insights into what the LORD does with His name for the good of His people. This a meaty, satisfying read, one that I will be treasuring and pondering in my heart for years to come.

KATIE SCHUERMANN, AUTHOR

BLESSED BE HIS NAME

Revealing the Sacred Names of God

Kevin S. Golden

CONCORDIA PUBLISHING HOUSE • SAINT LOUIS

For Joy

The holiness of whose name
is exceeded only by the Lord's

Published by Concordia Publishing House
3558 S. Jefferson Avenue, St. Louis, MO 63118-3968
1-800-325-3040 • cph.org

Manufactured in the United States of America

1   2   3   4   5   6   7   8   9   10   30   29   28   27   26   25   24   23   22   21

TABLE OF CONTENTS

PREFACE

I do not recall when the repeated reference to the name of the LORD in Scripture and the Church's liturgy first caught my attention. Now, my ears perk up and my eyes open all the wider any time the name of the LORD is mentioned. That is the source of some pain because the name of the LORD is typically used in a disrespectful manner in this age. The world uses the name of the LORD as an expletive, a curse, something to express shock or disgust; He uses His name as a blessing, an invitation, the embodiment of love, His own presence.

Many books have been written about the meaning of the various names and/or titles that the LORD uses in Scripture. This book approaches the name of the LORD from another scriptural angle: What does the LORD bind to His name, and what does He do with His name? Those are the questions addressed by this book.

There are many articles in scholarly reference works that deal with the topic of this book. In the following pages, I bring that discussion to those who are not familiar with the biblical languages. This tome does not provide an exhaustive treatment of what the LORD reveals about the content and use of His name. There is always more bound up in His name and then given to us. This is an introduction; it

> **What does the LORD bind to His name, and what does He do with His name?**

should enlighten minds with the beauty of the name of the LORD and encourage them to study Scripture to learn more of His name. Likewise, the brevity of this book is testament to the fact that the great truths are simple yet profound rather than complicated and shallow.

While my target is lay theologians, I pray that professional theologians might also benefit from this book. Due to my focus upon lay theologians, I have largely omitted the biblical languages and technical terminology, and all biblical references are to the versification found in English translations rather than the original languages. (Unless otherwise noted, English translations herein are from the English Standard Version.) But when one is dealing with a topic as deeply profound as the name of the LORD, Greek and Hebrew terms cannot be fully absent. If any who know the biblical languages are interested in chatting with me about this topic with the languages in view, I am happy to do so.

Speaking of the languages, I follow standard conventions for bringing the personal name of God into English. The personal name of God—the Hebrew name יהוה—will be indicated in the text of this book as "LORD" (notice the capitalization of the letters). You will read this when Old Testament texts are being quoted and when I am referring to the name of the LORD. You will not find the capitalized form when New Testament texts are being used, as biblical Greek did not utilize the name "Yahweh." There will also be occasions when the Old Testament text will use "Lord GOD." The Hebrew text there has "Lord Yahweh," so rather than a redundant expression "Lord LORD," the divine name is written as "GOD."

Some of the material contained within this book was field-tested during Sunday morning Bible study with the members of the congregation to which I have been called—Village Lutheran Church in Ladue, Missouri. I have benefited not only from the opportunity to flesh out some ideas in their presence but also from their feedback. A decade has passed since the Sunday-morning

Bible study series that gave birth to this book. It is because of the encouragement of members that it has not taken longer for this book to be written.

I also give thanks to those who have blessed my name. My parents gave me the Golden surname, a name of which I need not be ashamed. They also instilled in me a self-discipline that has enabled me to live a life that I pray is worthy of that name. My wife granted me the highest human honor by taking my name as her own, thus completing me. Our seven children now bear our surname as a blessed proclamation of the union that Christ has worked in us.

The highest thanks belong to the God who has revealed Himself in the name of the Father, Son, and Holy Spirit. He blessed me by placing His name upon me in Holy Baptism. He has written my name in His Book of Life. He has allowed me the privilege of hearing the proclamation of His name in Scripture. He has promised that I shall rise again on the Last Day that I might sing the praise of His name for all eternity.

Introduction

A brother pastor was listening to a talk radio station while driving between appointments. In exasperation, the host blurted out, "Christ!" He was not referring to the God revealed in Scripture. "Christ" was nothing more than an expletive, a means to express surprise or anger. With righteous indignation, the pastor contacted the station to inform them that the host's language was offensive to him and others who call upon the name of the LORD.

The station's response referenced Federal Communications Commission (FCC) regulations that list offensive words that are prohibited from being spoken on the air. Christ was not on that list and so they believed the host had done no wrong. The obvious deduction is that governmental laws are the final authority. If the government is fine with it, then it is fine.

This did not satisfy my reverent brother pastor so he pressed further. "Would the radio host consider using the term Allah in such a flippant way? Wouldn't that offend the Muslim audience and thus be out of bounds? Since the misuse of Christ is offensive to Christians, shouldn't there be an on-air apology?" The station replied that an apology was not warranted, because, after all, Christ is "just a word, just a name."

Just a name.

Are names so inconsequential that we may treat them as throwaway words? I have yet to meet someone who would not be offended if his own name were treated that way. Hit your thumb with a hammer. "Oh, Kevin; that hurts!" You see a couple exceeding the bounds of discretion with their amorous actions. "For Kevin's sake! Have they no shame?" Your favorite team is clinging to a lead and they bring in a struggling reliever who you know will blow the lead like he has so many other times this season. "O my Kevin!" At first, using my personal name in that way appears comical. Yet it does not take long before it becomes tired at best. In short order, it becomes downright offensive. I have invested a lot in my name in the hope that when people hear my name they think positively. By my actions, I have sought to invest confidence, trust, and honor in my name. Were my name used as an expletive, my investment would be not only denied but also turned on its head as my name becomes shorthand not for integrity but for scorn and disdain.

If that is true for me, a sinner, it is all the truer for the LORD. He is quite serious about His name. You can see it in the Second Commandment: "You shall not take the name of the LORD your God in vain" (Exodus 20:7).[1] This commandment, like all the others, is an extension of the First Commandment. To live by any of the commandments requires that we place no false gods before the one true God. Whenever any one of the commandments is broken, some false god has been placed before the one true God. Luther's Small Catechism teaches this truth. It explains the First Commandment: "We should fear, love, and trust in God above all things." The Small Catechism echoes this in its explanation of the remaining commandments, each of which begins, "We should fear and love God so that . . ." The First Commandment is the sum and focus of all the commandments. The other commandments

---

[1] The original text of Scripture does not number the Commandments, and there are some Christian confessions that number the Commandments differently. What Lutherans recognize as the Second Commandment some refer to as the Third. Their alternate Second Commandment is the LORD's rejoinder against fashioning idols. Lutherans see this as part of the First Commandment rather than a separate commandment. Those who list it as an independent commandment often do so because of an objection to visual representations of Christ (crucifixes, icons, mosaics, and the like).

are simply the means by which the First Commandment is lived out. It is telling that the LORD gives priority to the honoring of His name as He lists the various means by which He is put first in one's life. The Second Commandment takes priority over the remaining commandments.

The LORD's concern that His name be honored is further seen in the original giving of the Ten Commandments in Exodus 20. There one reads, "You shall not take the name of the LORD your God in vain, for the LORD will not hold him guiltless who takes His name in vain" (Exodus 20:7). The command is repeated verbatim in Deuteronomy 5:11. This is the only commandment to which the LORD attaches His specific warning that the offender will not be held guiltless. The Lord further instructs His people that swearing falsely by His name profanes His name (Leviticus 19:12). Because of the severity of taking His name in vain, the punishment for blasphemy of His name was death (Leviticus 24:16). The LORD further proclaimed that the prophet who falsely prophesied in His name was to be put to death (Deuteronomy 18:20). Such an abuse of the name of the LORD was especially troublesome because He had promised to send One who would speak in His name (Deuteronomy 18:18–19). This tension between the One promised by the LORD to speak in His name and the death sentence to be exacted upon the one who falsely prophesied in His name became enfleshed in the life of Christ. He is the fulfillment of the promise, but He was not recognized as such. And so Christ was routinely accused of blasphemy (Mark 2:7), and it was upon the false charge of blasphemy that Jesus was declared worthy of death (Matthew 26:65–66). In His every thought, word, and deed, Christ handled the name of the LORD with the greatest gravity. To take God's name in vain is to treat it as nothing, a throwaway word, "just a name." Christ does the opposite. He bears the name in every ounce of His being with due respect.

In His own teaching, Christ further underscores the importance of honoring the name of the LORD. When He teaches His disciples to pray, the first petition He offers is "Hallowed be Your name" (Matthew 6:9; Luke 11:2). We have the privilege of approaching God with our every concern. Jesus teaches us to pray to "Our Father" so that we may ask Him as dear children ask their own dear father. With boldness, we can and should ask Him to meet our physical needs ("Give us this day our daily bread"). With confidence, we can and should ask Him to work forgiveness in our life ("Forgive us our trespasses as we forgive those who trespass against us"). Without hesitation, we can and should ask Him to keep us from temptation ("Lead us not into temptation"). Without fear, we can and should ask Him to save us from all that could harm us ("Deliver us from evil"). It is an honor to be able to approach the King of kings with these and many other requests. Yet Christ teaches us that the hallowing of His name is of first importance. Just as the ordering of the commandments places the honoring of the name of the LORD as the first means of living in reverence toward Him, so also the Lord's Prayer teaches us by its order that the LORD's name takes precedence among the petitions. Thus, Luther writes: "In this petition God becomes everything and man becomes nothing. The other six petitions

> **"You shall not take the name of the LORD your God in vain, for the LORD will not hold him guiltless who takes His name in vain" (Exodus 20:7).**

serve the same purpose and intent, namely, the hallowing of God's name."[2]

The LORD calls us to honor His name, but our sinful nature drives us to do the opposite. It is so commonplace for His name to be taken in vain that it has even lost its shock value for many. While my brother pastor took note of the misuse of Christ's name by a radio host, there was no indication that anyone joined him in voicing offense at such a treatment of Christ's name. It is likely that the abuse of Christ's name did not even register with many listeners who are so accustomed to hearing such perverse speech that they do not notice when it happens.

The normalization of the misuse of God's name is apparent in the sports world. The major professional sports leagues have adopted player conduct policies that include punishment for offensive language. Thus, a player in the NBA may be subject to a fine of $50,000 for making a homophobic slur. Yet that same player can be heard taking God's name in vain without even a warning being issued.

The advent of social media has further normalized disrespect for God's name. With three quick keystrokes, many choose to express their surprise or anger with "OMG." Though some may protest that they were intending an innocent "Oh my goodness," "Oh my God" is the oft-assumed meaning of the shorthand. Such abuse of God's name results from laziness in finding an appropriate means to express surprise. Honoring God's name, on the other hand, involves discipline, using a word in accord with its purpose and meaning. Dishonoring God's name requires no discipline. Use a word contrary to its purpose and meaning and, suddenly, rather than having a specific meaning, a word is

---

2   Martin Luther, *An Exposition of the Lord's Prayer for Simple Laymen (1519)*, Luther's Works, American Edition: vol. 42 © 1969 by Fortress Press, p. 27. Used by permission.

cheapened to mean so much more than it was ever intended to mean. Using it to mean more causes it to mean less.

Such disrespect for God's name ought not surprise us. Why would God's name be respected by us when we don't respect our own names? Professional athletes sign their names to contracts to play for a specified period of time for a specified amount of money. A particularly productive season will often lead those athletes to hold out for a new contract. Why should he settle for $1 million per year when he is performing at the same level as another athlete making $2 million per year? And so he justifies the holdout and, in the process, makes public proclamation that he values an extra million dollars more than the sanctity of his own name. Once again, this age has accustomed us to dishonoring our own names. Breaking a bond that has been sealed with one's name cheapens the name, yet it happens regularly. It is seen quite clearly when legal contracts are not honored. But our names may be dishonored by other means as well. Giving our names in membership to an organization puts us in line with that organization's values. The one who guards the sanctity of his name will guard it from association with those organizations of spurious values.

By our own actions, our names are oft dishonored. We would do well to hearken to the wisdom set forth in the Book of Proverbs, where it is written, "A good name is to be chosen rather than great riches" (Proverbs 22:1; cf. Nehemiah 6:13 and Isaiah 65:15). If we treasured our names more than our money, we would all be much richer. This proverb speaks of one's name as one's reputation. A good reputation is preferable to great riches. Luther's Small Catechism confesses this truth in its explanation of the Fourth Petition of the Lord's Prayer. There we read: "Daily bread includes everything that has to do with the support and needs of the body, such as . . . good reputation." Asking the Lord to provide our daily bread includes asking Him to protect our name that we might have a good reputation. The chief means by which the Lord protects our name is by leading us to live in such a manner that our actions do not bring us into disrepute.

What Christ gives in the Lord's Prayer is also taught in the Ten Commandments. The Lord's gift of daily bread via a good name is protected by His commandment that "You shall not give false testimony against your neighbor." Much is protected by that command, not the least of which is your name and reputation as well as your neighbor's. Luther's Small Catechism explains the commandment, saying, "We should fear and love God so that we do not tell lies about our neighbor, betray him, slander him, or *hurt his reputation*, but defend him, *speak well of him*, and explain everything in the kindest way" (emphasis added). While the prohibition against hurting our neighbor's reputation is about guarding his name, the command to "speak well of him" calls us to build up one another's name.

> "A good name is to be chosen rather than great riches" (Proverbs 22:1).

In a similar way, Shakespeare put the following words into the mouth of Thomas Mowbray: "Mine honour is my life; both grow in one. Take honour from me, and my life is done."[3] A good name is the product of a good reputation, which brings honor to the name. Dishonor does violence to a good name. When a good name is destroyed by honor being taken away, then life itself has been lost.

I treasure even more the wisdom of Lutheran pastor and hymnwriter Paul Gerhardt. In the twilight years of his life, he wrote his last will and testament to his sole surviving son (he had four other children whom he outlived as they fell prey to disease).

---

3   William Shakespeare, *Richard II*, Act I, Scene 1.

Gerhardt's last will and testament includes these profound words: "To my only son whom I am leaving behind, I will bestow on him very little worldly goods, but at the same time an honorable name of which he will never need to be ashamed."[4] Gerhardt's son received the greatest of riches from his father: an honorable name.

There is good reason for each of us to guard our name, but there is even more reason to revere God's name. His name is to be adored because He has packed a lot into it and He does a lot with it. Strictly speaking, His name is Yahweh. While "God" is a title, Yahweh is God's personal name. The name Yahweh is used throughout the Old Testament, including the Second Commandment: "You shall not misuse the name of Yahweh, your God." In order to ensure that the divine name Yahweh was not misused, the practice arose not to speak the divine name. Instead, whenever "Yahweh" was seen in the text of the Old Testament, the Hebrew word *Adonai* was vocalized. Since *Adonai* means "lord," English translations have replaced "Yahweh" with "the Lord." The reader can discern that "Yahweh" is present in the original text by the translator using small capital letters in the font for "the Lord."

While Yahweh is God's personal name, He chooses to use many other titles ("God," "Lord," "Savior," etc.) and names (Jesus, Immanuel, etc.). It is not the name Yahweh alone that is to be honored, but each of the names or titles that Yahweh appropriates to Himself. I have never heard someone abuse "Yahweh," but many other biblical names and/or titles for God are regularly abused. From "OMG!" to "Good Lord!" to "Jesus Christ!" to "God damn!" to "For Christ's sake!" Through the poverty of human discourse,

Yahweh is God's personal name.

---

4   This is the author's translation of text in *Paul Gerhardt und seine Leider* by Jörg Erb, © 1974 Neuhausen-Stuttgart.

Yahweh is regularly disrespected as the names and titles that He has chosen for Himself are treated with disrespect.

To this point, I have given more attention to the regular abuse of God's name than to its blessing. That will now change. This introduction has been heavy on Law that calls us to repent for our sinful misuse of God's holy name as well as our abuse of our own names and our neighbor's name. It is time for Gospel. The rest of this book is focused upon everything that the LORD does for us and gives to us through His name as He has promised in Scripture. That is why we revere His name—because it is full of grace and blessing. Reverence for His name is not driven by terror over the consequences of not honoring that name. Reverence for His name is driven by awe that He would pile so much into His name and then give it to us. When the LORD reveals to you all that He has for you in His name, then the fit reaction of faith is to proclaim, "Blessed be the name of the LORD!"

Study Questions

1. How does the Second Commandment illustrate the importance of the name of the LORD?

2. What does it mean to take God's name in vain? How should we handle His name?

3. How does Christ teach us that the hallowing of the name of the LORD is of first importance?

4. Discuss the discipline that is necessary to honor God's name (and our own names, for that matter).

5. What are the merits of using God's personal name, Yahweh? What are the merits to using "the LORD" as a substitute for His name?

What's in a Name?

Juliet:

O Romeo, Romeo! wherefore art thou Romeo?
Deny thy father and refuse thy name;
Or, if thou wilt not, be but sworn my love,
And I'll no longer be a Capulet.

Romeo:

[Aside] Shall I hear more, or shall I speak at this?

Juliet:

'Tis but thy name that is my enemy;
Thou art thyself, though not a Montague.
What's Montague? it is nor hand, nor foot,
Nor arm, nor face, nor any other part
Belonging to a man. O, be some other name!
What's in a name? That which we call a rose
By any other name would smell as sweet;
So Romeo would, were he not Romeo call'd,
Retain that dear perfection which he owes
Without that title. Romeo, doff thy name,
And for that name which is no part of thee
Take all myself.

Romeo:

I take thee at thy word:
Call me but love, and I'll be new baptized;
Henceforth I never will be Romeo.[5]

The haunting words of star-crossed lovers Romeo and Juliet are etched in the lore of English literature. Theirs would be a happy tale but for one fact: their names are incompatible. The Capulets and Montagues do not mix. And so, a happy romance becomes a tragedy. Juliet recognizes the core of their problem, so she cries out, "Deny thy father and refuse thy name." She continues, "'Tis but thy name that is my enemy," and, "O, be some other name!" The challenge of the family name is summed up in her question and her own answer: "What's in a name? that which we call a rose by any other name would smell as sweet."

Romeo takes Juliet at her word, swearing off his name that he might be baptized into another name, the name of love. Yet they cannot escape their names. It is not that easy to rid ourselves of the identity that attaches to us by virtue of our name, especially a war-torn history of a long-standing surname. Names are powerful. They carry meaning. Romeo and Juliet do not escape their tragic end, because they cannot escape their family names.

Shakespeare's beloved play is testament to the meaning packed into names. The Bible goes even further in the significance that it attaches to names. Whereas it is family allegiance and interfamily violence that has been imputed to Romeo and Juliet, the Bible testifies to names that not only define a person in connection to others but also define him or her personally and, most important, in relationship to God. The significance of names in Scripture may be seen in Ecclesiastes 7:1: "A good name is better than precious ointment." Precious ointments, like gold or silver, could be used

---

5   William Shakespeare, *Romeo and Juliet*, Act II, Scene 2.

as a commodity, while also serving a useful purpose in a harsh environment. Even still, something so valuable is to be set aside in favor of a good name.

Such wisdom begs for our honor. Since the fall into sin, every age has succumbed to greed, seeking that which moth and rust shall destroy rather than that which will last into eternity. Names last. Long after a man has died, his name lives on in memory. Even more, the names of the faithful are written in the Lamb's Book of Life, carrying their names into eternity. But the value of a good name is not simply about its perpetuity. Within Scripture, a good name has value for the present as well as the future.

— Names Reflect Reality —

One reason for a good name being valued in Scripture is that names reflect the reality of what is named. There was a time when this was true in our culture, at least when it came to family names. In the age when sons followed in the same occupation as their father, the family name would reveal the family business. The Smith family worked as blacksmiths. The Miller family operated a mill. Today in our society, family names do not reveal our occupation. At best, family names reveal part of one's ethnic heritage. My family name—Golden—is an Irish name, which is but a small part of my lineage. Other Irish names carry further meaning. If my surname were *O'Golden*, it would mean "of Golden." If my surname were *MacGolden*, it would mean "son of Golden."

Personal names reveal even less about a person. The only thing you can learn of me from the name Kevin is that I am a male. But then there are those names that do not reveal a person's sex. The name Chris could be short for Christopher or Christine. Pat could be either Patrick or Patricia. And then there are those names that are unisex even before abbreviation—Shannon, Morgan, Taylor. Also present among us are those whose names are unique enough that they reveal nothing about the person other than their parents' contempt for convention—Apple, Suri, Audio Silence, Billion, Blanket, Kulture, Java. Other parents choose names that are virtues that they wish to instill in their child—Joy, Hope, Faith, Pax. I was blessed to serve as pastor for a man named Virtus. He went by Vic, but he lived up to his given name. *Virtus* is the Latin root for "virtue." More specifically, *Virtus* means "manliness" (*vir* is Latin for "man"). He exhibited true manliness, not as society typically defines manliness but in a far more positive sense. He was a faithful husband, father, and servant of Christ.

Scripture invests names with much more meaning. A person's name, especially with Hebrew names, reflected who he or she was. The first human, Adam, was given a name derived from the Hebrew word for "earth," *Adamah*, for he was created from the dust of the earth. The second human, Eve—or *Chavah* in Hebrew—was given a name from the Hebrew word for "life," as she is the mother of all the living. A short list of other names, far from exhaustive, illustrates how Hebrew names reveal personal identity.

NAME	MEANING
Noah	Peace
Abraham	Father of many nations
Sarah	Princess
Isaac	He laughs
Jacob	He grabs the heel; he cheats
Leah	Weary (drawn from Akkadian word for "cow")

NAME	MEANING
Rachel	Ewe
Israel	He strives with God
Moses	Drawn out
Joshua	Yahweh is salvation
Hannah	He [God] is gracious to me
Samuel	Heard by God
Elisha	My God saves
Elijah	My God is Yahweh

Not only are personal names invested with meaning in Scripture; place names are as well. For example, as Jacob flees for his life from Esau, the LORD delivers to him a dream in which a ladder connecting heaven and earth appears, with angels ascending and descending upon it. Upon awaking, he names that place Bethel, saying, "Surely the LORD is in this place" (Genesis 28:16). *Bethel* is the perfect name for that place, as it means "house of God." Later in life, Jacob would have another nighttime encounter with God. In this incident, he would wrestle with God, who renamed him to be Israel. Israel names that place Peniel, saying, "I have seen God face to face" (Genesis 32:30). *Peniel* translates as "face of God." From both personal names and place names, it is apparent that in Scripture, names are not trivial but carry significant meaning that reflects the reality of the person or thing that is named.

— Naming as an Act of Authority —

The act of naming carries significant weight in Scripture, not only in that the given name defines a person, but also that the person doing the naming is exercising authority over the person or place being named. Thus, it was commonplace for kings to rename conquered cities and captured individuals, both as an act demonstrating their authority over the renamed and as an attempt to redefine the person or place. Adam's authority over the animals is seen in his naming of all of them (Genesis 2:19). The LORD's authority over Jacob is seen in His renaming Jacob to be Israel (Genesis 32:28).

In Scripture, names are not trivial but carry significant meaning.

A king's authority over a conquered land, the LORD's authority over Jacob/Israel, and Adam's authority over the animals is one thing. Some take offense, however, when they read of Adam naming Eve (Genesis 3:20), thus exercising his authority over her. Believing the exercise of authority to be the action of a superior over a subordinate, some look with umbrage upon Adam's naming authority over Eve. That offense dissolves when authority is understood biblically.

Two matters are key to understanding biblical authority. First, authority does not necessarily define one person as superior to another. Certainly, the LORD is over and above all others. Adam, Eve, and their descendants are over and above the rest of creation. But what of the Father and the Son? Repeatedly, Christ makes it apparent that He is under the Father's authority, obeying His will. The most dramatic example of Christ submitting to His Father's authority is His prayer in Gethsemane, when He asks to be spared the cup. His submission to the Father's authority is undeniable as He prays, "Not My will, but Yours be done" (see Matthew 26:42). The Father's authority over the Son, however, does not mean His superiority to the Son. Christ is equally adamant in His proclamation that He and the Father are equals, that they are one (John 10:30, et al.). Thus, Adam's authority over Eve does not mean his superiority. In fact, the text is rather clear that Adam and Eve are equals. She is made from Adam's side. She is of the same stuff as Adam; she is his equal. There is an order within each of these relationships of equals. The Father has authority over His equal, the Son. Adam has been given authority over his equal, Eve.

> **I nam'd them, as they pass'd, and understood**
> **Their nature, with such knowledge God endued.[6]**

Adam was able to name the creatures because he understood their nature. When the Lord God brings the woman to the man, Adam simply calls her "woman." English fails to capture the profundity of Adam's naming. In Hebrew, *man* (as in *male*) is *ish*. Adam calls her *ishah*, which is the word *man* with a feminine ending. She is the same as him, his equal, for they bear the same name. But his name is masculine in form and hers is feminine in form because they are complementary equals. Later Adam will call her *Eve*, Hebrew for "mother." The one thing he can understand about her is that she is the mother of all the living. His naming does not so much define her as it describes her. He cannot define her because she is beyond his ability to understand.

Still, a man's authority over his wife creates challenges. The Father is perfect and holy, and thus He will not abuse His authority over the Son. Man is not perfect and is given to abusing his

---

6   John Milton, *Paradise Lost*, Book VIII, lines 352–53.

authority. Thus, there is an ever-present need for Christ's teaching regarding authority. For sinful humans, authority is oft perverted into a power play, the ability to establish the rules and to enforce the rules. Sinners think in terms of hierarchy, with the one on top domineering those underneath. Whether in the home, the workplace, or any other relationship, it is customary to expect the one with authority to wield it for his own benefit. That is not a biblical handling of authority. Consider Adam and Eve, with their authority over creation. Authority is specifically given by God so that man might care for creation (Genesis 2:15). Man's authority is as caretaker, not as abuser.

Again, this truth is most poignantly captured in the words of Christ (Matthew 20:25–28). He reminds His disciples that the world's way of doing authority is for the one with authority to lord it over others. To this Christ replies, "It shall not be so among you." How shall it be? Authority shall be about service, the greatest being a servant and the first becoming a slave. The definition of such authority is found in Christ, who is greatest and first and yet becomes slave and servant of all by giving His life as a ransom. Biblical authority is not domineering; it is serving. Living by biblical standards, to name someone is to exercise authority over that person by putting his or her needs above your own.

> There is an ever-present need for Christ's teaching regarding authority.

Apply that to today's naming rites. Though the practice is not as prevalent as in former generations, it is still common for a woman to take the family name of her husband. For Christians, significant biblical teaching is tied up in the woman's new name. It signals that the man is the head of the woman, that he has authority. What does that authority mean? That he will serve her, that her needs are to come before his own, that he even views her as greater than himself. His calling to serve her is to be modeled after Christ's authority over His Bride, the Church, which led Him to lay down His life for her (Ephesians 5:25–27). Christ sets the standard for the husband providing for and protecting his bride as most precious.

Less troubling to modern ears is the naming of children. The parents' authority over the child is seen both as they name the child and as the child takes their family name. Parental authority does mean that they establish rules for proper conduct and enforce those very rules. Yet it does not mean domineering control over the child. Parents can all reflect honestly upon their experience as a child and as a parent, leading them to recognize that faithfully living as a parent according to God's calling involves sacrifice. Children may complain about the demands of the chores given to them by their parents, but it is parents who give of their time, energy, and financial resources for the sake of their children.

> **To name someone is to exercise authority over them by submitting to their needs taking precedence over your own.**

— Names as Personal Identity —

The significance of names in Scripture has already been established for various reasons, including that names give definition to the ones who bear them. It is commonplace for those names to be loaded with theological meaning. In other words, the saints of old received their first and central identity from the LORD. For example, the prophet Elijah's name means "My God

is Yahweh." Not only does his name define him according to the
Lord, but it also sets him in his role as the Lord's spokesman
against the worship of Baal and Asherah, sponsored by King
Ahab of Israel and his notorious wife Jezebel. From Elijah, the
reader without knowledge of Hebrew can still acquire the means
to see the presence of the divine in many biblical names. The
El of *Elijah* comes from the Hebrew word for "God." Consider
all the biblical figures whose names include *El*—*El*isha, Dani*el*,
Gabri*el*, Ezeki*el*. The *jah* of *Elijah* is an abbreviation of God's
name Yahweh, which English transliteration also abbreviates
in other ways, including Ah. A few of the names that have
an abbreviation of *Yahweh* within them are Isai*ah*, Jeremi*ah*,
Obadi*ah*, Zephani*ah*, and Zechari*ah*. The reader should beware
that not every appearance of *el* in a name translated into English
is evidence of "God" in the Hebrew. Even more, not every *ah* is
evidence of "Yahweh" in the Hebrew name, as *ah* is the common
ending for a feminine noun. Nevertheless, the examples offered
above illustrate the divine significance of biblical names.

A heart-wrenching example of the Lord using names as His
means to communicate is found in the life of the prophet Hosea.
The Lord called this prophet to be a living object lesson of His
people's unfaithfulness. As the Lord's relationship with His
people is often described as the relationship between bridegroom
and bride, the unfaithfulness of His people would be described
in terms of prostitution. Thus, Hosea is called by God to marry a
prostitute. The prophet's unfaithful wife is a public proclamation
of the unfaithfulness of the Lord's people. Hosea's unfaithful wife
gives birth to two children whom the Lord commands Hosea
to name Lo-Ammi and Lo-Ruhammah. *Lo-Ammi* translates to
"Not My people," underscoring the Lord's judgment upon His
unfaithful people. *Lo-Ruhammah* translates to "No compassion"

to emphasize the LORD's wrath against their sin. Powerful names they are, but not ones we would want to repeat!

Fortunately, by end of Hosea's prophecy, there is promise of restoration for the unfaithful people of God who have repented of their unfaithfulness. That promise brings the reader to recall the Word of the LORD found in Isaiah 62:1–5, in which He promises that He will give His people a new name. No longer shall they be called "Deserted" or "Desolate," but "My delight is in her" and "Married." Those beautiful names in Hebrew are *Hephzibah* and *Beulah*, respectively. While they are not commonplace today, they carry a load of goodness.

Much of what has been said to this point about the significance of biblical names is encapsulated in the lives of Hananiah, Mishael, and Azariah. Their names are not familiar to many. Most know them as Shadrach, Meshach, and Abednego, but in everlasting life you will call upon them as *Hananiah, Mishael,* and *Azariah.* These lesser-known names are good Hebrew names that can be translated as "Yahweh is gracious," "Who is what God is?" and "Yahweh is my help." These three young men were taken into exile in Babylon, along with their friend Daniel (Hebrew for "God is my judge"). They are brought into the service of King Nebuchadnezzar, whose servant summarily renames them (Daniel 1:7), including Daniel (whose new name is Belteshazzar).

The renaming takes place for two reasons. First, it demonstrates Nebuchadnezzar's authority over them—they will be answerable to him! Second, he is seeking to redefine them. Their Hebrew names defined them according to the LORD. Their new Babylonian names are not entirely clear, but each refers to a Babylonian god. They are being called away from fidelity to the LORD to serve idols. Each of them famously rejects this redefinition, living up to his Hebrew name. The threesome of Hananiah, Mishael, and Azariah chose the fiery furnace over denying the LORD, who saved them (Daniel 3). Daniel has more widespread influence, including his refusal to give up his daily discipline of prayer. Thus, he is thrown into the lions' den, where he survives the night thanks to Lord's intervention (Daniel 6).

— The Name and the Presence of the Lord —

The weight of biblical names is impressive. While human names bear great weight, the Lord's use of His own name is even more striking. God chooses to make Himself inseparable from His name. It is commonplace within the Psalms for the Lord's name to be set in parallel with the Lord Himself, thus making the two indistinguishable so that the Lord's name is made the object of the praise that is given to the Lord Himself. The following are but a few examples of this phenomenon.

> Oh sing to the Lord a new song;
> sing to the Lord, all the earth!
> Sing to the Lord, bless His name;
> tell of His salvation from day to day.
>
> *(Psalm 96:1–2)*

> Enter His gates with thanksgiving,
> and His courts with praise!
> Give thanks to Him; bless His name!
>
> *(Psalm 100:4)*

> Bless the Lord, O my soul,
> and all that is within me,
> bless His holy name!
>
> *(Psalm 103:1)*

I will extol You, my God and King,
and bless Your name forever and ever.

(Psalm 145:1)

My mouth will speak the praise of the LORD,
and let all flesh bless His holy name forever and ever.

(Psalm 145:21)

The simple point drawn from this bond between the LORD and His name is that He is present wherever His name is found. This is not only true for the triune God in general but specifically for Christ as well. When the apostles are arrested and brought before the governing authorities on account of their proclamation of Christ, we read that they were "rejoicing that they were counted worthy to suffer dishonor for the name" (Acts 5:41). Here "the name" stands in for "Jesus" or "Christ." Similarly, John describes those who labor for Christ as those who "have gone out for the sake of the name" (3 John 7). Once again, reference to Christ is made by simply stating "the name," for where His name is, He is.

> **God chooses to make Himself inseparable from His name.**

This reality has led the faithful to find confidence in the name of the LORD. When in need of strength, they trust in His name. "Some trust in chariots and some in horses, but we trust in the name of the LORD our God" (Psalm 20:7). Again, "Our help is in the name of the LORD, who made heaven and earth" (Psalm 124:8). Because "the name of the LORD" is the object of trust and the source of help, the faithful set up their banners in His name as they rejoice in His salvation (Psalm 20:5). The establishment of banners is strong warfare imagery akin to present-day troops raising their flag. The might of the name of the LORD delivers the certainty of victory to His people so they set up their banners even before the battle has been won, because victory is assured. Warfare language again emerges as the psalmist proclaims, "Through Your name we tread down those who rise up against us" (Psalm 44:5). When surrounded by an enemy swarming like bees and going out with the ferocity of fire racing through thorns, the one who trusts in the LORD is confident. The enemy is defeated because "in the name of the LORD I cut them off!" (mentioned three times for emphasis in Psalm 118:10–12).

Such warfare language emphasizes that the LORD is not only present in His name but that He is also present *for you* in His name. The LORD employs His name on behalf of His people. That is why it was so common, and even a great joy, for the faithful to have personal names that included reference to God or Yahweh. That is why the faithful would praise His name, for it was and remains the means by which He fights for His people. His name is His gift to His people by which He dwells among them that He might serve them, providing for and protecting them, thus fulfilling His position of authority.

The coming chapters will unfold how the LORD acts for you in His name. In anticipation of the discussion of the coming chapters, rejoice in the gift of His name by virtue of its specificity. We may casually speak of knowing someone by name. With the weight that is packed into names within Scripture, to know somebody by name is to know that person intimately and specifically. God has made Himself known to you by His name Yahweh. That is a precious gift in an age in which God is often described in anonymous terms to encapsulate the vagaries of the religious smorgasbord set before our society.

> The LORD employs His name on behalf of His people.

An anonymous god is no god at all, for it is undefined and unable to be found. An anonymous god dwells in shadows, never being revealed. But the one true God has made Himself known by virtue of His name. With that name, He blesses you. In that name, you can trust, for in that name, He is present *for you.*

Study Questions

1. How do names reflect reality?

2. How is naming an act of authority?

3. How is authority abused? How is authority properly exercised?

4. If you have children, what did you name them? Why?

    If you do not have children, what would you name children? Why?

5. How does the reference to God within biblical names reflect the proper center of our lives?

6. Why is it significant that God is inseparable from His name? How is He "for you" in His name?

7. Think of a time you named something—a pet, a plant, a stuffed animal, a toy. How did the act of naming alter your attitude toward the named thing?

With God as My Witness: The Name of the Lord Delivering His Presence

"I don't believe you. You have promised time and again that you would get the job done and it hasn't happened. Actions speak louder than words, and your actions tell me that I cannot count on you."

"But this time is different! I am serious now. You know that before, I had a lot of growing up to do so I didn't follow through. Now I'm ready to do what I have to do."

"Fool me once, shame on you. Fool me twice, shame on me. Well, I've been shamed too many times by continuing to trust you. You've established a pattern that empty promises cannot erase."

"With God as my witness, I won't fail you this time."

Calling upon God as a witness is often a last-ditch plea to be taken seriously. God is treated as a tool to gloss over past wrongs. The LORD certainly forgives our sin, but that does not erase the temporal consequences of our choices. "With God as my witness" is a bargaining chip to up the ante for the seriousness of one's commitment. Though uttered frequently, it is an irreverent use of God's name because it treats His name flippantly. One thing it gets right is that God is present. Wherever God's name is found, He is present. But to what end is He present? "With God as my witness" acts as if His presence can be used as the speaker desires. But speaking God's name does not grant you control over Him. Quite the opposite; in speaking God's name, you are putting your trust in what He has promised to do with His presence. God is present, not only in terms of His omnipresence (God is unbounded by location and so is present in all places), but also very specifically as He makes Himself known by virtue of His name. Wherever His name is present, He is personally present. He reveals Himself by His name.

God is so intent upon connecting with His people that He uses His name as a theophany, the self-revelation of God to humans. Such manifestations are found throughout Scripture. Scriptural accounts of theophany utilize some standard elements. Often God manifests Himself on a mountaintop. On Mount Sinai, the LORD speaks to Moses, calling him to go to Egypt because the LORD will use him to set His people free (Exodus 3). The LORD again speaks to Moses on Mount Sinai while the people of Israel wait at the base of the mountain (Exodus 19). It is on Mount Carmel that the LORD manifests Himself in Elijah's contest with the prophets of Baal (1 Kings 18). On the Mount of Transfiguration, Christ gives Peter, James, and John a glimpse of His glory (Matthew 17; Mark 9; Luke 9).

There on the Mount of Transfiguration, Christ shines forth, displaying another standard element of a scriptural theophany—light. Paul is given a theophany on the road to Damascus, being blinded by the light of Christ (Acts 9). Often the light of a theophany comes from fire. It is specifically fire that is sent by the LORD to consume Elijah's sacrifice before the prophets of Baal on Mount Carmel. The LORD appears to Moses from fire within a bush, yet the bush is not consumed by the fire. The LORD leads His people out of Egypt by means of a pillar of cloud by day and a pillar of fire by night (Exodus 13:21).

> **Speaking God's name calls upon you to trust in what He has promised to do with His presence.**

The ultimate theophany is the incarnation as God takes on human flesh. Jesus is fully divine and fully human, a mystery that fulfills and transcends all other theophanies. Thus, it is fitting that the incarnation is intimately tied to the name of the LORD, a matter that will be discussed in the chapter entitled "O Jesus Christ: The Name of the LORD Fulfilled in Jesus."

— The Name of the LORD Engenders Fear —

God's presence via His name can be frightening. When the LORD allows Moses to look upon His glory (albeit only His back) and reveals Himself to Moses by proclaiming His name, He calls Moses, Israel, and all the faithful to reverent fear. He speaks words reminiscent of the giving of the Ten Commandments (Exodus 20:5), that He "will by no means clear the guilty, visiting the iniquity of the fathers on the children and the children's children, to the third and fourth generation" (Exodus 34:7). Due fear is also delivered through Isaiah, who declares, "Behold, the name of the LORD comes from afar, burning with His anger, and in thick rising smoke; His lips are full of fury, and His tongue is like a devouring fire" (Exodus 30:27).

Deuteronomy 28:58–59 and Psalm 61:5 pointedly capture the LORD's teaching that His name is to be feared. In the former, Moses instructs God's people that in observing His Word, they fear His name. Moses further warns them that if they do not so fear His name and observe His Word, then He will bring punishment upon them. Whereas Moses warns, David promises. In Psalm 61:5, David promises the heritage that is given to those who fear the name of God.

The LORD calls us to fear His name and so fear Him. Yet fear is not popular. We take the edge off of fear by speaking of it in terms of reverence and awe. While reverence and awe before the LORD are certainly right, the fear of the LORD and His name includes even more than that. True fear before Him results from the recognition that I am a sinner and that He is present in His name. As a sinner, I fear the just condemnation of the LORD.

Fear also has a very positive component. Psalm 130:3–4 rejoices in the forgiveness found in the LORD, which prompts true fear. Fear results from forgiveness? Yes, because His forgiveness reveals just how different He is from us. We make a list and check it twice when others offend us. The LORD does not. Instead of marking iniquities, He forgives. What kind of LORD is this that He should so delight in forgiveness? One around whom I cannot wrap my mind because He does not act the way that I do. And because He is so different and His ways so distinct from our own, fear results in a very positive sense. We fear what we do not understand.

Much about the LORD and His name escapes our understanding because He is God and we are not. In theology, we describe this with the Latin term *Deus absconditus*, "the hidden God." True knowledge of God is dependent upon *Deus revelatus*, "the revealed God," who makes Himself known in His name through Holy Scripture. Even this revealed knowledge of God leaves us scratching our heads. What kind of LORD delights in forgiveness rather than marking iniquities? He is beyond my comprehension, and so fear results.

— God's Personal Name —

Moses knew the fear of God. In Exodus 3, God appears to Moses, speaking to him from the burning bush. Moses rightly hides his face out of fear (Exodus 3:6). God then tells Moses why He is appearing to him: He has heard His people's cry and He will deliver them from slavery in Egypt. Moses will be His chosen instrument to accomplish their deliverance. This is no light task. Egypt is a political and military powerhouse.

Moses objects, first asking, "Who am I that I should go to Pharaoh and bring the children of Israel out of Egypt?" (Exodus 3:11). God's response is simple: "I will be with you" (Exodus 3:12). Moses further objects that when he tells the people of Israel that the God of their fathers has sent him, they will ask, "What is His name?" So, God reveals His name to Moses.

God responds, "I AM WHO I AM. . . . Thus, you will say to the sons of Israel, 'I AM' has sent me to you" (Exodus 3:14, author's translation). In the very next verse, God further instructs Moses, saying, "Yahweh, the God of your fathers, the God of Abraham, the God of Isaac, and the God of Jacob, has sent me to you" (Exodus 3:15, author's translation).

God reveals His personal name. His name is Yahweh. You will find variant spellings of that name as it is brought from Hebrew into English. Since biblical

> **God reveals His name to Moses . . . "I am who I am."**

Hebrew was written without vowels, some choose to bring God's personal name from Hebrew into English by transliterating the four consonants of His name as YHWH.

What is lost in translation is the relationship between God's self-identification as "I am" and as "Yahweh." Hebrew verbs utilize prefixes to indicate a change in person (I vs. you vs. he/she/it) and number (I vs. we; you vs. you all; he/she/it vs. they), among other things. The verbal root remains the same as the prefix changes to indicate the person and number. "I am" and "Yahweh" utilize the same verbal root with a change in the prefix. Instead of "I am," "Yahweh" would be rendered "He is."

This rather simple explanation of God's personal name, Yahweh, is far from exhaustive of the linguistic discussion of the name. It makes sense that when God refers to Himself as "I am," we would then refer to Him as "He is." But what does that mean? In part, it means that God is ever beyond our ability to comprehend. After all, He wouldn't be much of a God if I could wrap my mind around Him. Nevertheless, He chooses to reveal specific things about Himself through His name.

First, He reveals His personal name so that you might call upon Him. That is among the great blessings of knowing another's name. You can call upon someone by name even as you can speak of the person by name. Luther's Small Catechism teaches this in the explanation of the Second Commandment, which is concerned about the proper use of the name of the LORD. Why is it given to us? That we may "call upon it in every trouble, pray, praise, and give thanks."

God also tells Moses that His name, Yahweh, is His memorial. Specifically, God says, "This is My name forever and this is My memorial from generation to generation" (Exodus 3:15, author's translation). What does it mean for God's name, Yahweh, to be His memorial? Many translations render this verse so that His name is how He is to be remembered. That is certainly part of what it means for "Yahweh" to be His memorial. A few other texts help reveal more. Isaiah 26:8 ties God's name and His memorial together as the desire of His people. Psalm 135:13 poetically places the name of the LORD and His memorial (some translations use "renown") in parallel, a standard means by which Hebrew poetry identifies two things with each other. Proverbs 10:7 also uses parallelism to tie a person's name with memorial. Yet it is not God's name and memorial that Proverbs has in view but that of the righteous and the wicked. Hosea 12:5 takes us back specifically to the name of the LORD as His memorial name.

These texts illustrate that the name of the LORD is more than simply the means by which you remember Him. His name carries His renown, His reputation (more about that later in this book). It also bears His very being. You cannot separate the LORD from His name. And in His name you are taught His character, what makes the LORD to be the LORD, what sets Him apart from everyone else, what makes Him to be God unlike any god, what makes Him holy—distinct, different, unique, separate from all others, what He does for you and for all.

— The Creed of Creeds —

God would again reveal Himself to Moses on Mount Sinai by proclaiming His name. A great deal had transpired since God revealed His name, Yahweh, in Exodus 3. Moses went to Egypt with greats signs and wonders that the LORD delivered through his hands. There were ten plagues, the last of which finally convinced Pharaoh to let God's people go. The Passover was given as the LORD's means of saving the faithful from the tenth plague. After Pharaoh had changed his mind and sent his chariots after the people of Israel, the LORD was present among His people as a pillar of cloud by day and a pillar of fire by night. At the sea, the LORD parted the waters so that the people of Israel walked through on dry ground, while the waters came crashing back down on Pharaoh's army. The LORD then further provided for His people by giving them manna, bringing water from a rock, and turning bitter water sweet. Eventually, in accord with the LORD's promise, they arrive at Sinai. There the LORD gives His ten statements (often referred to as the Ten Commandments), along with other instructions and promises. The covenant is confirmed at Sinai as well. Initial instructions and provisions for the tabernacle are given by the LORD to Moses.

Much of this is given by the LORD to Moses while he is on the mountain, away from the people of Israel and in the presence of the LORD. The glory of the LORD is upon the mountain in a cloud (Exodus 24:15–16). To the people, the glory of the LORD appeared as a consuming fire upon the mountain (Exodus 24:17). Moses remains there for forty days—more than enough time for the people of Israel to be overtaken by idolatry. They make a golden calf and bow down to it. The LORD is rightly incensed at their idolatry. He tells Moses to leave Him alone so that His wrath may burn against them and consume them (Exodus 32:10). Instead,

Moses intercedes for Israel. His intercession is not grounded upon their worthiness, as if they deserved to be spared. Instead, Moses calls upon the LORD to spare Israel for the sake of His promise to their forefathers (the LORD always keeps His promises) and for the sake of His own reputation (Exodus 32:11–14).

Israel is spared by the LORD's mercy. Still, Moses is greatly distressed. He throws down the stone tablets, upon which are written the LORD's ten statements, so that they shatter. Moses seeks consolation by requesting that the LORD show him His ways (Exodus 33:13). The LORD does even more than that. The LORD reveals Himself, His very character, by proclaiming His name to Moses. The LORD tells Moses, "I will make all My goodness pass before you and will proclaim before you My name 'The LORD.' And I will be gracious to whom I will be gracious, and will show mercy on whom I will show mercy" (Exodus 33:19). There He gives a glimpse into what is packed into His name, namely, His grace and mercy. What the LORD promises to reveal He unveils in even grander fashion in the coming verses.

And it all happens as He proclaims His name. He reveals Himself by His name because His very self is packed into His name. "The LORD descended in the cloud and stood with him there, and proclaimed the name of the LORD. The LORD passed before him and proclaimed, 'The LORD, the LORD, a God merciful and gracious, slow to anger, and abounding in steadfast love and faithfulness, keeping steadfast love

> **The LORD reveals Himself, His very character, by proclaiming His name.**

for thousands, forgiving iniquity and transgression and sin'" (Exodus 34:5–7a). Packed into His name are three couplets that define His character. He is "merciful and gracious." He is "slow to anger, and abounding in steadfast love and faithfulness."

He "[keeps] steadfast love for thousands, [and forgives] iniquity and transgression and sin." Couplets are common in Hebrew. That there are three couplets is also not surprising, as the Lord delights to do things in threes.

In His self-revelation via His name, the Lord also states that He "will by no means clear the guilty, visiting the iniquity of the fathers on the children and the children's children, to the third and fourth generation" (Exodus 34:7b). It is telling that rather than three couplets, this statement of Law comes as a single item. The Lord leads with His gracious character while the Law remains present. This is often described as the difference between God's proper and alien works. His proper work—what He delights to do, what is central to His character—is graciously forgiving us. His alien work—what He does because it is in keeping with His justice—is judging the guilty. One of the great benefits of His alien work and His revelation that He "will by no means clear the guilty" is that we are guarded from cheap grace, which sees His mercy and forgiveness as an excuse to continue in sin.

There is much to be learned from this account. One lesson flows from Moses' reaction. Upon the Lord revealing Himself via His name, "Moses quickly bowed his head toward the earth and worshiped" (Exodus 34:8). More accurate than "worshiped," Moses prostrated himself before the Lord. How do you respond to the presence of the Lord? Moses' posture shows humility. It is proper that we respond in like fashion when the Lord's name delivers His presence to us. Moses' faithful response is echoed by many today who bow their head in humility at the mention of God's name, whether it be the triune name, the name of Christ, or any other name by which the Lord chooses to make Himself known.

A second lesson is found in the ongoing usage of the Lord's self-revelation. "The Lord, the Lord, a God merciful and gracious, slow to anger, and abounding in steadfast love and faithfulness, keeping steadfast love for thousands, forgiving iniquity and transgression and sin" is a creed. Creeds begin with divine self-revelation—God tells us who He is and what He does. Then the faithful repeat that self-revelation for a variety of reasons. Repeating what He has revealed of Himself firmly sets the truth within the faithful. It further serves to pass the faith to the next generation as well as to others. Furthermore, it teaches the faithful what to expect out of God. Expect Him to act according to what He has revealed about Himself. Ask Him to act according to what He has revealed about Himself. When need prompts you to turn to the LORD in prayer, your desires will not give you confidence. Confidence will only be found in what is certain and sure. You bank on what He has revealed about Himself.

That is how the faithful utilized "The LORD, the LORD, a God merciful and gracious, slow to anger, and abounding in steadfast love and faithfulness, keeping steadfast love for thousands, forgiving iniquity and transgression and sin." It is the "Creed of creeds" within the Old Testament. "Creed of creeds" is the grammatical means within Hebrew to express the superlative. In English, we typically add -*est* to the end of a word or use the helping word *most* to express the superlative. Hebrew superlatives take the form "x of x." "King of kings" means the kingliest of all. "Holy of holies" means the holiest space. This is the "Creed of creeds"—that is, the greatest creed,

> God tells us who He is and what He does. Then the faithful repeat that self-revelation for a variety of reasons.

as it is repeated fourteen times in the Old Testament. Sometimes it is abbreviated, which is not surprising, as it was commonplace for a single phrase to be used to evoke an entire text. Whether abbreviated or not, this creed is repeated in contexts where the focus is upon the LORD's gracious self-revelation as the ground for confidence. You find that in the following texts:

- Numbers 14:18—Moses intercedes on behalf of Israel on the basis of what the LORD has placed in His name lest He wipe out rebellious Israel.

- Deuteronomy 4:31—Knowing that Israel will fall prey to idolatry in the future, Moses promises that the people will return to the LORD due to His character as revealed in His name.

- 2 Chronicles 30:9—Hezekiah anticipates that the LORD will receive His people back due to His character as revealed in His name.

- Nehemiah 9:17, 31—The Levites, collectively on behalf of Israel, recall why the LORD spared their forefathers: namely, due to His character as revealed in His name.

- Psalm 78:38—The psalmist recalls why the LORD spared Israel in the desert due to His gracious character.

- Psalm 86:5, 15—David prays for deliverance based upon who the LORD is as revealed in His name.

- Psalm 103:8—David offers the LORD's character as revealed in His name as the reason to bless His holy name (v. 1).

- Psalm 111:4—In this psalm of praise, the psalmist lists the gracious character of God as revealed in His name as reason for praising the LORD.

- Psalm 112:4—In another psalm of praise, the LORD's gracious character is recalled.

- Psalm 116:5—Within a prayer for deliverance, the psalmist finds confidence in the gracious character of the LORD.

- Psalm 145:8–9—In yet another psalm of praise, David finds good reason for praise in the gracious character of the LORD.

- Joel 2:13–14—The prophet calls the LORD's people to repentance, giving good reason for them to return to the LORD: namely, His character as revealed in His name.

- Jonah 4:2—The prophet reveals why he resisted going to Nineveh, knowing that the LORD would rather spare Nineveh than destroy them because of His character as revealed in His name.

- Nahum 1:3—Though Nineveh was spared destruction at the time of Jonah, Nahum proclaims the LORD's judgment upon Nineveh because His gracious character does not allow the guilty to live in impenitence.

— Cause My Name to Dwell There —

The LORD invests Himself in His name. And He delivers it to His people concretely. Having created His people as flesh and blood, the LORD makes Himself present in very physical means. He promises, "In every place where I cause My name to be remembered I will come to you and bless you" (Exodus 20:24).

In other words, the Lord is present wherever His name is found. You cannot separate the Lord from His name.

Among the blessings flowing from this promise is certainty. The Lord does not deal with us in the way of doubt. He grants us unwavering confidence by giving us concrete specificity. That is found in His name and in His choosing to locate His name in very specific places. So He directs Moses to instruct His people that they are not to worship the Lord wherever they might desire, but they are to "seek the place that the Lord your God will choose out of all your tribes to put His name and make His habitation there" (Deuteronomy 12:5). Lest His instruction not be heard, He repeats the same truth in short order regarding the specific location of sacrifices, saying, "Then to the place that the Lord your God will choose, to make His name dwell there, there you shall bring all that I command you: your burnt offerings" (Deuteronomy 12:11).

The Lord continues this teaching throughout the Book of Deuteronomy. He directs that tithes are not to be taken to any random location, but specifically "before the Lord your God, in the place that He will choose, to make His name dwell there" (Deuteronomy 14:23). He specifies that "you shall offer the Passover sacrifice to the Lord your God, from the flock or the herd, at the place that the Lord will choose, to make His name dwell there" (Deuteronomy 16:2; similarly in 16:6). So also, another festival, the Feast of Weeks, is to be observed as the faithful rejoice "at the place that the Lord your God will choose, to make His name dwell there" (Deuteronomy 16:11). Yet again, the Lord instructs His people that they are to offer the firstfruits of their harvest in the Promised Land in "the place that the Lord your God will choose, to make His name dwell there" (Deuteronomy 26:2).

Why such repetition about the LORD choosing where His name will dwell? For one, the LORD has authority over His own name. Nobody gets to run His name for Him. The LORD names Himself; He reveals Himself by His name (it is not discovered); He chooses where His name will dwell. His name will only be used to the ends that He promises. This is a reminder of the dangerous heresy found within the so-called Word-Faith movement. Perverting such passages as "If you ask Me anything in My name, I will do it" (John 14:14), the unsuspecting are sold a lie: if you call upon the name of Jesus and have sufficient faith, He will give you what you ask. This is to wrest the LORD's name from Him to control Him. But the LORD is not a vending machine so that you can put in the currency of His name and get out the product you desire. His name can only be utilized to the ends He has promised.

— Tabernacle and Temple —

The LORD is also consistent in proclaiming that His name will be found where He has chosen because He has chosen a specific place; namely, the temple in Jerusalem. During the days of Moses, the LORD established the tabernacle that was His chosen place to dwell among His people. He promised that the day was coming when the tent of the tabernacle would give way to the permanent structure of the temple. This is the background of Deuteronomy 12:11, where He says, "To the place that the LORD your God will choose, to make His name dwell there, there you

> The LORD names Himself; He reveals Himself by His name; . . . He chooses where His name will dwell.

shall bring all that I command you." Again, the worship of the LORD is not something that is from human invention. True worship follows what God promises in His Word. And what He promises is certain and sure, lest we doubt. So, He chooses a specific place for His name to dwell with all the grace and mercy that He packs into His name so that we have unwavering confidence.

Four centuries after Moses, the LORD would tell David that his son was the one chosen by the LORD to build the temple. The LORD says to David of his son, "He shall build a house for My name, and I will establish the throne of his kingdom forever" (2 Samuel 7:13). The initial fulfillment of this promise is found in Solomon whom the LORD uses to construct the temple. Solomon knows the promise attached to the temple as the locale of the LORD's name. At the dedication of the temple, he prays:

> "But will God indeed dwell on the earth? Behold, heaven and the highest heaven cannot contain You; how much less this house that I have built! Yet have regard to the prayer of Your servant and to his plea, O LORD my God, listening to the cry and to the prayer that Your servant prays before You this day, that Your eyes may be open night and day toward this house, the place of which You have said, 'My name shall be there,' that You may listen to the prayer that Your servant offers toward this place. And listen to the plea of Your servant and of Your people Israel, when they pray toward this place. And listen in heaven Your dwelling place, and when You hear, forgive."
>
> *(1 Kings 8:27–30; see also 2 Chronicles 6:18–21)*

Will God dwell on earth? It makes no sense that the One who holds all creation in His hand would dwell in a specific place in

His creation. Yet He does that very thing because He has chosen to do so. He does it in His name. And He does it because He is gracious, so that He has a place at which forgiveness is given out. The LORD assures Solomon (and you) that this is true. "And the LORD said to [Solomon], 'I have heard your prayer and your plea, which you have made before Me. I have consecrated this house that you have built, by putting My name there forever. My eyes and My heart will be there for all time'" (1 Kings 9:3).

The faithful took hold of this promise. Before battle, King Jehoshaphat prays to the LORD that He spare Jerusalem because in it is a sanctuary for His name (2 Chronicles 20:8). The prophet Isaiah regularly extols the beauty of Zion, the specific mount upon which the temple was built. He also knows that Zion is not great because of physical grandeur but because it is the "place of the name of the LORD of hosts" (Isaiah 18:7). The psalmist also calls the LORD to defend His sanctuary because it is "the dwelling place of Your name" (Psalm 74:7). The LORD set His name in the temple, and so He was there with His grace.

Despite the LORD's great promise, Solomon falls prey to temptation. The LORD's just punishment for Solomon's sin is that the kingdom is divided. Yet even as the kingdom splits, the LORD promises that He will preserve Jerusalem, the location of the temple, where He has chosen to put His name (1 Kings 11:36). In time, Jerusalem would be overthrown, the temple razed, and the LORD's people exiled. When the LORD restores His people, Nehemiah knows why. He prays to the LORD that He allow him to gather His people back on the basis of His own promise to bring His people "to the place that I have chosen, to make My name dwell there" (Nehemiah 1:9).

But what of the LORD's promise to David regarding his son? David's son was to build the temple, and his kingdom was to last forever. Solomon's temple was leveled, his kingdom was split in the very next generation, and eventually his line lost the kingship. Is the LORD not faithful to His promise?

Yes, He is faithful. His promises find their fulfillment in Christ. He is the Son of David (Matthew 1:1). The LORD promised that His name would dwell in the tabernacle and temple. All of that is funneled right into Jesus. "The Word became flesh and tabernacled among us and we beheld His glory, glory as of the only Son from the Father, full of grace and truth" (John 1:14, author's translation). Jesus is where the LORD tabernacles among us with grace. Jesus says, "Destroy this temple, and in three days I will raise it up" (John 2:19). He is not speaking of the grand building on Mount Zion. "He was speaking about the temple of His body. When therefore He was raised from the dead, His disciples remembered that He had said this, and they believed the Scripture and the word that Jesus had spoken" (John 2:21–22). Jesus is the temple where the name of the LORD dwells among us with grace, mercy, and forgiveness. As Jesus is the fulfillment of all God's promises, He is the fullness of the name of the LORD. Far more will be said of this blessed truth in a subsequent chapter. For now, rejoice that Christ is tabernacle and temple. That means God dwells with His people. He is for you!

Study Questions

1. What do *Deus absconditus* and *Deus revelatus* mean? In which do we find true knowledge of God?

2. What is a theophany? How do theophanies invoke righteous fear?

3. Why does God reveal His personal name?

4. God reveals Himself to Moses by His name. That revelation demonstrates His proper and alien works. What is His proper work? What is His alien work?

5. How does God's self-revelation by His name serve as a creed?

6. Jesus is the fulfillment of the tabernacle and temple. Why is this important?

By God: The Legal Use of God's Name

> "It occurred to me that I need to call my brother and sister so we can discuss what we're doing for Mom and Dad's anniversary. We only have a year and half to put everything together."
>
> "What do you mean, a year and a half? You don't have that much time. You've only got six months."
>
> "By God, you're right!"

It is common in American parlance to add God's name to add emphasis without adding any meaning to what is said. God, on the other hand, adds a great deal by means of His name. When He places His name upon something, He is making a legal claim to it. It has been said that possession is nine-tenths of the law. Yet when it comes to divine legal claim to someone by placing His name upon that person, far more than nine-tenths of the law is involved. Indeed, God placing His name upon you is full-fledged Gospel. It does call upon you to live as one who belongs to God, but you belong to God even when your behavior does not match that reality.

— Naming Your Possessions —

When God places His name upon something, He is claiming ownership. We do much the same thing. Children write their name on their toys. Book lovers inscribe their name with joy inside the cover of a newly purchased tome. When I was in grade school, my mother would painstakingly write out my name countless times on paper, cut them out, and then tape my name to every pencil, pen, and crayon, lest another claim what she had purchased for me. Our claim to what bears our name diminishes over time. Children outgrow their toys. Book lovers allow books to collect dust and eventually part with them. But when God places His name upon something, He pledges to cherish it forever as His beloved possession.

In the biblical world, speaking your name over something constituted an official legal act of transferring property or claiming ownership. The biblical examples are manifold, including when human possession is indicated by placing one's name upon another. In 2 Samuel 12:28, Joab encourages David to take the city of Rabbah. Joab has been besieging the city on behalf of David but does not want to complete the conquest lest it be called by his name rather than David's. Joab knew that the city would belong to the one whose name was upon it. A similar but far darker example is found in Isaiah 4:1, where Isaiah foretells the coming judgment upon Jerusalem that would include the annihilation of the male fighting populace.

> **When God places His name upon something, He is claiming ownership.**

As a result, he says, the days will be so harsh that seven women will take hold of one man, all asking to be called by his name. In an age when women had little legal standing of their own accord, seven women all asking to bear the name of the same man bespeaks their desperation. While our society provides women their own standing apart from men, this is a reminder that one of the blessings of marriage is care and provision.

Biblical Wisdom Literature often contrasts the wise and the foolish. The former listen to instruction, heed God's Word, and humble themselves before God. The latter spurn instruction, ignore God's Word, and exalt themselves before others. Psalm 49:11 presents wisdom in a rather sobering fashion by noting that the wise and the foolish are alike in that both die, even though "they called lands by their own names." Both wise and foolish accumulate great possessions, but death is no respecter of possessions. Place your name upon possessions, accomplishments, and more, yet death still comes. This truth cannot be denied. It can crush even the heartiest. Thus, it leaves us longing for One who can name and take hold forever, even in death.

The LORD places His name upon any number of items and persons, claiming them as His own and revealing that He cherishes the named item or person. In 2 Samuel 6:2, the ark of the covenant is called by the name of the LORD of hosts. The ark had been constructed according to God's instruction given in Exodus 25. It held the stone tablets upon which the LORD had given Moses the Ten Commandments, Aaron's staff that had budded in Numbers 17, and a jar of manna. These testified to God's provision for His people during their desert wanderings and beyond. The lid of the ark was called the Mercy Seat, for there the LORD dwelt in mercy for His people, dispensing forgiveness. There was no doubting to whom the ark belonged, for it bore the name of the LORD of hosts. It was His for the purpose He promised: mercy.

The instructions for the ark were given to Moses. It would be more than four hundred years before the temple would be built by Solomon. The innermost part of the temple would house the ark with the Mercy Seat of God, and so that innermost part of the temple would be called the Holy of Holies [ESV: Most Holy Place]. It is not surprising that the temple also bears the name of the LORD. In 1 Kings 8:43, Solomon prays at the dedication of the temple, saying, "This house that I have built is called by Your name." Again, there is no doubt to whom the temple belongs and for whose purposes it is to be used. It bears the name of the LORD.

Yet it is not just things that bear the LORD's name. Solomon's prayer at the dedication of the temple is also recorded in 2 Chronicles. There Solomon refers to the people of the LORD being called by His name (7:14). The significance is great. For one thing, bearing the name of the LORD should inform the people how they are to conduct themselves. Even more, bearing His name gives them promise that the LORD will hear their prayers and come to their aid when they call upon Him. Bearing the name of the LORD means that they are His cherished possession. He cannot help but care for them.

The prophet Isaiah captures the beauty of bearing the name of the LORD from a different angle. His people's suffering is captured with the words of Isaiah 63:19: "We have become like those over whom You have never ruled, like those who are not called by Your name." To not be called by the name of the LORD is to be robbed of His goodness, His love, His mercy, His presence. Being called by His name is placed alongside living under His rule. The LORD is not an autocratic dictator but the selfless, serving King of kings.

The prophet Jeremiah also picks up on the significance of bearing the name of the Lord. First, he delivers the Word of the Lord that calls His people to account for profaning His temple: "Has this house, which is called by My name, become a den of robbers in your eyes?" (Jeremiah 7:11; see also vv. 10, 14). The Lord will not tolerate the misuse of what bears His name. He will not tolerate the abuse of the temple and so He brings judgment upon Jerusalem since it bears His name by virtue of being the locale of the temple. Through Jeremiah He says, "For behold, I begin to work disaster at the city that is called by My name, and shall you go unpunished?" (Jeremiah 25:29). The Lord's judgment is graphically described as the cup of His wrath. As intoxication lays the drunkard low, so the cup of His wrath overwhelms. "Thus says the Lord of hosts, the God of Israel: Drink, be drunk and vomit, fall and rise no more, because of the sword that I am sending among you" (Jeremiah 25:27). The Lord is serious about His name because His name bears His very presence; His name makes us His.

While the Lord will not tolerate our abuse of those things that bear His name, the Lord also saves those who bear His name. So we hear from Daniel, who dwells in Babylon along with the exiled people of Jerusalem. Daniel calls upon the Lord to deliver His people from exile that they might be set free to return home. He prays, "O my God, incline Your ear and hear. Open Your eyes and see our desolations, and the city that is called by Your name. For we do not present our pleas before You because of our righteousness, but because of Your great mercy. O Lord, hear; O Lord, forgive. O Lord, pay attention and act. Delay not, for Your own sake, O my God, because Your city and Your people are called by Your name" (Daniel 9:18–19). Daniel honestly assesses that the city and the people are not worthy to be saved. But he knows the Lord's mercy and banks on it. He further grounds the LORD's mercy upon the people and the city bearing His name. To deny them would be to deny His own name. There is much we can learn from Daniel about how to pray. Prayer takes hold of Christ's promises, and it finds confidence in the name of the LORD given to us in Holy Baptism. The LORD cannot ignore us, because we bear His name. To ignore would be to deny His own name, something He cannot do. Though He will not grant my requests that are contrary to His will, He will pay heed to prayer offered up by one who bears His name.

> The LORD also saves those who bear His name.

The temple and Jerusalem bore the name of the LORD. But He would not restrict His name to a few. He would have all bear His name that all might belong to Him and trust in Him. Thus, the prophet Amos promised that the day would come when the LORD would raise up the booth of David (a promise that was fulfilled in Christ) so that Israel may possess "all the nations who are called by My name" (Amos 9:12). This can be more precisely translated as "all the Gentiles who are called by My name." Israel, the people of God, was called to embrace all peoples, for the LORD sets His name upon all people from all nations.

— Baptismal Naming —

That the LORD will place His name upon people from all nations is evident in Christ's institution of Holy Baptism. Having won salvation by His cross and having risen from the grave in victory over death, Jesus calls His disciples and says, "Make disciples of all nations" (Matthew 28:19). Christ is inclusive in this calling. He places no qualifiers upon all nations—no ethnic restrictions, no age restrictions, no restrictions at all. He leaves it wide open because He would have all to be His disciples. And Jesus tells us how disciples are made: by baptizing and teaching. He makes disciples of all nations by baptizing them in the name of the Father and of the Son and of the Holy Spirit. In Baptism, the LORD puts His name upon us, and so we are His.

The LORD puts His name upon us in Baptism as our parents put their name upon us at birth. I was named Kevin at birth because my parents chose that name. I was given the surname Golden because that was my parents' name. Bearing their name and being named by them means that I belong to them. That means it is my calling to honor them. The blessings of belonging to faithful parents are far greater than the responsibility of honoring them. On the other hand, the right of parents to name a child carries great responsibility. Having named a child, parents cannot walk away from the child. They are responsible for the child, to provide for him or her physically, emotionally, academically, and spiritually. This is all the truer when it comes to being a child of God. In Baptism, you were adopted as a child of the Father when He placed His name upon you. The Father has only one begotten Son, our Savior, Jesus Christ. But in Baptism, countless are adopted as they receive His name. As His child, you are called to honor Him. Far greater is the privilege that is yours in having the Father take responsibility for you. He has authority over you and so you are called to follow His Word. Yet His authority over you also ensures His protection of and provision for you. Authority and provision are the flip side of the same reality.

What Christ delivers to all nations in Holy Baptism had been promised long ago. Through Moses, He promised, "All the peoples of the earth shall see that you are called by the name of the LORD" (Deuteronomy 28:10). The LORD intended for all to see His provision for His people through the exodus and into the Promised Land that all might also trust in Him. Even greater weight comes with the Word of the LORD through the prophets. Isaiah looks beyond Israel to "everyone who is called by My name, whom

> **The LORD puts His name upon us in Baptism.**

I created for My glory, whom I formed and made" (Isaiah 43:7). Notice the connection between creation and redemption. The LORD has created all for His glory; He has formed and made them. Thus, He also desires to call them all by His name that they might be saved. Isaiah further delivers the Lord's commitment to saving all by placing His name upon them as He proclaims, "I was ready to be sought by those who did not ask for Me; I was ready to be found by those who did not seek Me. I said, 'Here am I, here am I,' to a nation that was not called by My name" (Isaiah 65:1).

The LORD seeks all that all might bear His name. And what a name it is! James speaks of "the honorable name by which you were called" (James 2:7). By virtue of your Baptism, you bear the name of the LORD, an honorable name for which there is no shame. Because you bear such an honorable name, you can call upon the LORD with the same boldness as Jeremiah. He says, "Yet You, O LORD, are in the midst of us, and we are called by Your name; do not leave us" (Jeremiah 14:9). There is no doubt that the LORD dwells with you when He has placed His name upon you in Holy Baptism.

Listen again to Jeremiah, who was sore oppressed by those who refused to listen to the LORD. He calls out, saying, "O LORD, You know; remember me and visit me, and take vengeance for

> **By virtue of your Baptism, you bear the name of the LORD.**

me on my persecutors. In Your forbearance take me not away; know that for Your sake I bear reproach. Your words were found, and I ate them, and Your words became to me a joy and the delight of my heart, for I am called by Your name, O LORD, God of hosts" (Jeremiah 15:15–16). The prophet can rightly claim that when others reject him, they are rejecting the LORD, for the LORD called Jeremiah by His name. This is your confidence in the face of rejection and oppression. You are called by the name of the LORD. He dwells with you. What is done to you is not done in isolation; it is done to the LORD as well. He stands beside you to sustain you.

Study Questions

1. What sorts of things do you label with your name? Do you do this because of monetary or sentimental value?

2. In the biblical world, what was the significance of speaking one's name over something?

3. Upon what does the LORD put His name? What does this communicate?

4. "The right of parents to name a child carries great responsibility." Do you agree or disagree with this statement? Why?

5. How does Scripture connect creation and redemption?

For Christ's Sake: God's Name, Honor, and Reputation

"You'll have to do that again. That will never pass inspection."

"What are you talking about? That is how we always used to do it. It worked for years; it will work fine now."

"You know that code has changed, and for good reason. We are not going to cut corners when it comes to the safety of our customers."

"So I've wasted my whole day because you are going to be uptight about something that wasn't an issue five years ago?"

"Yeah, five years ago we didn't know any better. But the industry has improved in that time. We have improved as well. You know how we updated our procedure on this two years ago. If you don't want to do it right, then you can find a new job."

"For Christ's sake! You've got to be kidding me."

The epitome of taking the LORD's name in vain is when it adds no meaning to what you say other than shock value. But when something truly is done "for Christ's sake," a great deal of meaning is added. Christ's name bears His reputation and His honor. You may approach your work the same way. Knowing that your name is attached to what you have done, your reputation and honor are at stake. Repeatedly in Scripture, the LORD acts for the sake of His name because His reputation is at stake. This is similarly seen in Jesus' reputation preceding Him. King Herod, for example, heard of Jesus' ministry because His name had become known (Mark 6:14).

While a human's reputation is often tied to his name, the weight of the LORD's reputation being bound to His name is even more pronounced. After all, His name endures forever (Psalm 72:17). Since the LORD ties His honor and reputation to His name, His people have His name as the object of their love. So it is in Psalm 5:11: "Let all who take refuge in You rejoice; let them ever sing for joy, and spread Your protection over them, that those who love Your name may exult in You." Since the LORD acts for the sake of His name, "those who love His name shall dwell" in Zion (Psalm 69:36). This is also why the LORD will "turn to me and be gracious to me, as is Your way with those who love Your name" (Psalm 119:132). Those who convert to faith in the LORD "join themselves to the LORD, to minister to Him, to love the name of the LORD" (Isaiah 56:6).

— The Lord's Name and Reputation — in the Exodus from Egypt

Since the Lord's name carries what He has done, and thus His reputation, there is repeated reference to the Lord acting for the sake of His name when He delivered His people from slavery in Egypt. Amid the plagues that the Lord visits upon Egypt to convince Pharaoh to let His people go, He tells Moses why He is acting so mightily through him. He is raising up Moses "so that My name may be proclaimed in all the earth" (Exodus 9:16). The Lord would have all peoples know Him to be the God who saves those who trust in Him.

Israel struggles to trust that the Lord is such a faithful God. So when they arrive at the Promised Land, they refuse to enter and are ready to go back to Egypt. Despite the protestations of faithful Joshua and Caleb, they persist in their refusal to enter. The Lord tells Moses that He will disinherit Israel and make a nation of Moses that will be greater and mightier than Israel. Yet Israel is spared because Moses intercedes for them. His intercession is predicated upon the Lord's reputation: What will be said of the Lord? The nations, instead of trusting in His name, will say that He was unable to bring Israel into the Promised Land. For the sake of His name, Israel is spared.

> The Lord ties His honor and reputation to His name.

The Lord's gracious deliverance stood not only as a testament to the nations but to Israel as well. The generations that followed would remember the exodus as establishing the name of the Lord. Seven hundred years after the exodus, Isaiah recounts how the Lord worked through the hand of Moses and led them through the sea in order to make an everlasting and glorious name for the Lord (Isaiah 63:12, 14). Eight hundred and fifty years after the exodus, Jeremiah declares, "You have shown signs and wonders in the land of Egypt, and to this day in Israel and among all mankind, and have made a name for Yourself, as at this day" (Jeremiah 32:20). Nine hundred years after the exodus, Daniel pleads for the Lord's mercy by recalling, "O Lord our God, [You] brought Your people out of the land of Egypt with a mighty hand, and have made a name for Yourself" (Daniel 9:15). A millennium after the exodus, the people of Israel repent of their sin and recall the Lord's saving work, saying, "You saw the affliction of our fathers in Egypt and heard their cry at the Red Sea, and performed signs and wonders against Pharaoh and all his servants and all the people of his land, for You knew that they acted arrogantly against our fathers. And You made a name for Yourself, as it is to this day" (Nehemiah 9:9–10).

Man-on-the-street interviews reveal a shocking level of ignorance about our nation's history. Many cannot identify the general time frame of the U.S. Civil War. Others are not able to state the significance of the Fourth of July. Still more cannot name what happened on D-Day. And these are defining events for our nation within the past 250 years. Israel, on the other hand, regularly recalled what the Lord did in the exodus because it not only defined who they were but it also established the Lord's reputation. He made a name for Himself.

When the Lord acts for His name's sake, He is acting according to who He has revealed Himself to be. His name reveals His very nature. The exodus reveals He is a faithful God who remembers the promise He made to Abraham, Isaac, and Jacob, so that He acts to bring their descendants out of Egypt (Exodus 2:24). The exodus reveals that He is a saving God as He intervenes on behalf of His people so that they pass through the sea on dry ground. The exodus reveals that He is a gracious God so that He spares

His people when they rebel against Him. The LORD chooses to make Himself known by His name, and His name is defined by His actions. His reputation precedes Him because His actions have established His name.

This is true about the whole of the LORD's work on behalf of His people. It comes to its fullness in Christ, who is the embodiment of the name of the LORD. His actions leave no doubt regarding the LORD's reputation.

> **When the LORD acts for His name's sake, He is acting according to who He has revealed Himself to be.**

— The LORD's Concern for His — Name in the Prophets

The prophet Ezekiel gives attention to the Lord's concern for His name. The sin of His people had profaned His name, but the LORD will not suffer His name to be dishonored. So He says through Ezekiel, "I had concern for My holy name, which the house of Israel had profaned among the nations to which they came" (Ezekiel 36:21). Though their sin had dishonored His name, the LORD rises to defend its honor. Lest His people not hear Him, the LORD repeats that He acts for the sake of His name. In the span of fourteen verses, He states three times that He "acted for the sake of My name, that it should not be profaned in the sight of the nations among whom they lived" (Ezekiel 20:9, 14, 22). Not only does the LORD repeat that He acts for the sake of His name and reputation; He also repeatedly notes that He must do so because His people had profaned His name among the nations. They had publicly dishonored His name by refusing to live as His people. Rather than stick out as different and distinct, they had chosen to bow to cultural pressures, worshiping the gods of the nations.

There is nothing new under the sun. The same pressures that beset the LORD's people of old beset us now. As the world around us beckons us to mirror its values, the Church is called to honor the name of the LORD. We are called by His name. The LORD would have all bear His name, and so we seek to deliver His name to all. Still, bearing His name causes us to be different from the world. The nations are brought to the Church not by the Church mimicking the nations but by the Church showing forth the singular beauty of bearing the name of the LORD.

The Church is ever in need of repentance, both for our failure to reach out to the nations and for dishonoring the name of the LORD by mimicking the nations rather than remaining resolute in following the LORD. How does the LORD respond to our repentance? He acts to vindicate His holy name by cleansing us of our sin. Through Ezekiel, He declares:

> Thus says the Lord GOD: It is not for your sake, O house of Israel, that I am about to act, but for the sake of My holy name, which you have profaned among the nations to which you came. And I will vindicate the holiness of My great name, which has been profaned among the nations, and which you have profaned among them. And the nations will know that I am the LORD, declares the Lord GOD, when through you I vindicate My holiness before their eyes. I will take you from the nations and gather you from all the countries and bring you into your own land. I will sprinkle clean water on you, and you shall be clean from all your uncleannesses, and from all your idols I will cleanse you. And I will give you a new heart, and a new spirit I will put within you. And I will

remove the heart of stone from your flesh and give you a heart of flesh. And I will put My Spirit within you, and cause you to walk in My statutes and be careful to obey My rules. You shall dwell in the land that I gave to your fathers, and you shall be My people, and I will be your God.

(Ezekiel 36:22–28)

In shocking fashion, the LORD does not vindicate His name by crushing those who have profaned His name but by cleansing them of their sin. He does it for the sake of His name and for the benefit of His cleansed people and for the benefit of the nations who behold His gracious actions, thus knowing His name and reputation as a gracious God.

The LORD promises even more in this regard through Ezekiel. Again, He acts for the sake of His name so that more are drawn to Him. "My holy name I will make known in the midst of My people Israel, and I will not let My holy name be profaned anymore. And the nations shall know that I am the LORD, the Holy One in Israel" (Ezekiel 39:7). Furthermore, His saving acts grant a name to His people. Ezekiel 39:13 reports that the LORD, acting for the sake of His name, "will bring them renown on the day that I show My glory, declares the Lord GOD." The word translated as "renown" is the word for "name." His people's name, their reputation, flows from what the LORD has done on their behalf. And as if that were not enough, the LORD has more. "Therefore thus says the Lord GOD: Now I will restore the fortunes of Jacob and have mercy on the whole house of Israel, and I will be jealous for My holy name" (Ezekiel 39:25). He is jealous for His name. So what does He do? He restores His people. The LORD chooses to be known as the God who acts for the benefit of His people.

Ezekiel is not alone among the prophets in declaring that the LORD acts for the sake of His name. And again, the LORD acting for the sake of His name means He acts for the benefit of His people, namely, by withholding His anger over their sin: "For My name's sake I defer My anger" (Isaiah 48:9). Isaiah declares that the LORD not only withholds His anger for the sake of His name but also, for the sake of His name, He delivers manifold blessing. "Instead of the thorn shall come up the cypress; instead of the brier shall come up the myrtle; and it shall make a name for the LORD, an everlasting sign that shall not be cut off" (Isaiah 55:13).

Jeremiah follows suit. The LORD's name is so defined by His actions for the benefit of His people that He would have His people be His name. "As the loincloth clings to the waist of a man, so I made the whole house of Israel and the whole house of Judah cling to Me, declares the LORD, that they might be for Me a people, a name, a praise, and a glory" (Jeremiah 13:11). Our dependence upon the LORD reveals His name, a name of grace and mercy. Jeremiah learned this well so that he pleads with God that He forgive His people for the sake of His name: "Though our iniquities testify against us, act, O LORD, for Your name's sake . . . do not spurn us, for Your name's sake" (Jeremiah 14:7, 21). Calling upon the LORD to forgive for the sake of His name and despite our sin is familiar to those who have been well formed by the liturgy of the Church. The corporate confession of sin acknowledges that our sin leaves us unworthy of grace—"I, a poor, miserable sinner, confess unto You all my sins and iniquities with which I have ever offended You and justly deserved Your temporal and eternal punishment." So why would the LORD forgive us? We further confess, asking the LORD, "for the sake of the holy, innocent, bitter sufferings and death of Your beloved Son, Jesus Christ, to be gracious and merciful." With boldness and confidence in the name of the LORD, we ask forgiveness.

We bank everything on His reputation because His actions have established His renown.

To put it another way, we ask the Lord to be jealous. Just above we heard the words of Ezekiel 39:25, where the Lord said He is jealous for His name. This echoes the giving of the Ten Commandments, where the Lord says, "I the Lord your God am a jealous God" (Exodus 20:5). Even more profoundly, Exodus 34:14 speaks of "the Lord, whose name is Jealous." Your mother likely taught you that it is wrong to be jealous. In American parlance, *jealousy* has become interchangeable with *envy*, describing our desire for what belongs to another. Such desire is sinful. Yet in these biblical texts, "jealousy" describes the desire to keep what rightly belongs to you. There are occasions when such desire is sinful, such as when we choose to hoard our goods rather than help those in need. There are other settings in which jealousy—the desire to keep what rightfully belongs to you—is proper. Husband and wife are rightly jealous when they find another flirting with a spouse. Parents are rightly jealous when someone kidnaps their child. Even more, the Lord is rightly jealous when a false god would seduce His Bride, the Church, even snatching His children. His jealousy is seen in His application of the Law that demands that we forsake our false gods. His jealousy is seen even more in His forgiveness. He will not leave us in the clutches of sin and death. He acts for the sake of His jealous name and for our benefit, forgiving and restoring us.

— Dishonoring the Name of the Lord —

The Lord's gracious, saving acts are the motivation and means for us to live as His children, forsaking our idols. Even so, we struggle against our sinful nature. When we act contrary to His will—that is, contrary to His name that He has given us and contrary to His Word—His name is profaned. Earlier in this chapter, we heard the LORD's Word through Ezekiel that His name is profaned when His people do not live as He calls them to live (Ezekiel 36:20–21). Amos also speaks of the LORD's name being profaned by His people's sin: "Thus says the LORD: 'For three transgressions of Israel, and for four, I will not revoke the punishment, because they sell the righteous for silver, and the needy for a pair of sandals—those who trample the head of the poor into the dust of the earth and turn aside the way of the afflicted; a man and his father go in to the same girl, so that My holy name is profaned'" (Amos 2:6–7). To profane is to treat what is holy as if it were common. The LORD hallows His name; He sanctifies it for a unique purpose: namely, that we might call upon Him and declare Him to others. When we treat Him apart from the purposes for which He has given His name, He is treated as common rather than holy.

Our sin also defiles the name of the LORD (Ezekiel 43:8); that is, our sin dirties His name, for we bear His name. The sin of unbelievers does not defile His name to the same extent since they do not bear His name. Yet they sin against Him when they revile His name (Psalm 74:10, 18). The LORD's people are also guilty of despising His name when they do not call upon Him for aid as they should (Isaiah 52:5). The apostle Paul quotes this verse from Isaiah in Romans 2:24 to describe how the sin of God's people prompts unbelievers to blaspheme Him. There are many and various ways in which we dishonor the name of the LORD. The good news is that He honors His name by acting to save us. He is faithful to His name even when we are not.

> The LORD hallows His name; He sanctifies it for a unique purpose.

— The Lord's Honor in the Second — Commandment and the Lord's Prayer

Showing due honor to the name of the Lord is a Second Commandment issue. You shall not take the name of the Lord your God in vain. Living out this commandment is not only about refraining from abusing the name but also about using it properly. In paragraphs 54–55 of his treatment of the Second Commandment in the Large Catechism, Luther states:

> But the greatest abuse occurs in spiritual matters. These have to do with the conscience, when false preachers rise up and offer their lying vanities as God's Word.

> Look, all this is dressing up one's self with God's name, or making a pretty show, or claiming to be right. This is true whether it happens in common, worldly business or in higher, refined matters of faith and doctrine. Blasphemers also belong with the liars. I mean not just the most ordinary blasphemers, well known to everyone, who disgrace God's name without fear. (These are not for us to discipline, but for the hangman.) I also mean those who publicly disgrace the truth and God's Word and hand it over to the devil.

Luther does not take such abuse of the Lord's name lightly. He had learned well from Scripture that God and His name are inseparable, so to curse the name of the Lord is to curse the Lord Himself. Leviticus 24:11, 15–16 places blaspheming the name of the Lord parallel to (that is, identical to) cursing God. The same truth is taught in Revelation 13 as Christ reveals to John details about the beast out of the sea, which represents political tyranny. Again, blaspheming God is placed parallel to blaspheming His name (Revelation 13:6).

Luther takes this up again later in the Large Catechism's handling of the First Petition of the Lord's Prayer, "Hallowed be Thy name." Specifically, in paragraph 41, the catechism states that "God's name is profaned when people preach, teach, and say in God's name what is false and misleading. They use His name like an ornament and attract a market for falsehood. That is, indeed, the greatest way to profane and dishonor the divine name." Again, the focus is placed upon those who use the name of the Lord for purposes beyond His giving of the name.

Such misuse of the name of the Lord is akin to those building the tower of Babel who desire to "make a name for ourselves" (Genesis 11:4). Instead of the magnification of the divine name for the benefit of the Lord's people, false teachers magnify their own names for their own sake. A prime example is the Word-Faith movement, which claims that the Lord is beholden to grant what you request if you ask in His name with sufficient faith. Instead of magnifying the name of the Lord, He is diminished to be no more than a tool to be used to satiate your desires.

— Honoring the Name — of the Lord as Holy

Instead of being a means to another end, the Lord and His name are the *telos*, the end and goal, that Christians desire. Because He is the sum and focus of faith, and because He gives Himself to us in His name, His name is holy. In other words, His name is set apart for the purposes He has chosen. Here is a brief sampling of the texts that proclaim His name to be holy and how that impacts us.

Leviticus 20:3—"I will set My face against that man and will cut him off from among His people, because he has given one of his children to Molech, to make My sanctuary unclean and to profane My holy name."
His name is holy and so the abominable practice of sacrificing your child to an idol is intolerable.

Leviticus 22:32—"You shall not profane My holy name, that I may be sanctified among the people of Israel. I am the LORD who sanctifies you."
Since He makes us holy, we shall treat His name as holy, unique, set apart for the purpose of delivering Him to us.

1 Chronicles 16:10, 35—"Glory in His holy name; let the hearts of those who seek the LORD rejoice! . . . 'Save us, O God of our salvation, and gather and deliver us from among the nations, that we may give thanks to Your holy name, and glory in Your praise.'"
Because He saves us by His name, the LORD is due our thanks.

1 Chronicles 29:16—"O LORD our God, all this abundance that we have provided for building You a house for Your holy name comes from Your hand and is all Your own."
All good things come from Him and so He is worthy of receiving our best, especially when it comes to offerings dedicated to the proclamation of His holy name.

Psalm 33:21—"For our heart is glad in Him, because we trust in His holy name."
Because the LORD has set apart His name to deliver Himself to us, that name is worthy of trust.

Psalm 103:1—"Bless the Lord, O my soul, and all that is
within me, bless His holy name!"
Along with David, the whole of us is given to blessing
His name for all that He gives us through that name.

Psalm 105:3—"Glory in His holy name; let the hearts of
those who seek the Lord rejoice!"
Since the Lord is found in His name, that name
moves us to glorify Him.

Psalm 106:47—"Save us, O Lord our God, and gather us
from among the nations, that we may give thanks to
Your holy name and glory in Your praise."
His name is worthy of our praise because He saves us
by His name.

Psalm 145:21—"My mouth will speak the praise of the
Lord, and let all flesh bless His holy name forever
and ever." As we rightly praise His name, all people
are called to praise Him as well, for by His name He
works the salvation of all.

Isaiah 57:15—"For thus says the One who is high and lifted
up, who inhabits eternity, whose name is Holy: 'I dwell
in the high and holy place, and also with him who is
of a contrite and lowly spirit, to revive the spirt of the
lowly, and to revive the heart of the contrite.'"
By His holy name, He revives us. The paramedic does
not ask the dead man if he desires CPR but initiates
resuscitation of his own accord. So the Lord does acts
of His own initiative to revive us by His name.

Ezekiel 20:39—"As for you, O house of Israel, thus says the
Lord God: Go serve every one of you his idols, now
and hereafter, if you will not listen to Me; but My holy

name you shall no more profane with your gifts and your idols."

Because His name is holy, it cannot be set alongside our common idols.

Ezekiel 36:20–22—"But when they came to the nations, wherever they came, they profaned My holy name, in that people said of them, 'These are the people of the LORD, and yet they had to go out of His land.' But I had concern for My holy name, which the house of Israel had profaned among the nations to which they came. Therefore say to the house of Israel, Thus says the Lord GOD: It is not for your sake, O house of Israel, that I am about to act, but for the sake of My holy name, which you have profaned among the nations to which you came."

Even when our actions show disregard for His name, the LORD still acts for the sake of His name. Even when we treat His name as common, He treats His name according to its holiness. He is faithful to His name when we are not.

Ezekiel 39:7, 25—"And My holy name I will make known in the midst of My people Israel, and I will not let My holy name be profaned anymore. And the nations shall know that I am the LORD, the Holy One of Israel. . . . Therefore thus says the Lord GOD: Now I will restore the fortunes of Jacob and have mercy on the whole house of Israel, and I will be jealous for My holy name."

The LORD acts for the sake of His holy name for the benefit of His people who are restored and for the benefit of others who hear of Him that they might trust Him as well.

The Lord's name is holy; we are called to treat it accordingly. How might that be done? As the passages above illustrate, refraining from idolatry is of first importance. Yet all sin is idolatry. Whenever I sin, I break the First Commandment because I am setting some idol before the Lord. But these passages have also taught the Lord's concern for the contrite. Those who repent of their sin with due sorrow for their idolatry and with faith in the One whose name is holy are restored for the sake of His name. The name of the Lord is hallowed when we confess our sin and trust in His forgiveness.

Another means to hallow His name is our physical response. As holistic beings, what we do physically reflects, informs, and shapes the rest of our selves. We teach ourselves to hallow God's name when the mention of His name prompts us to bow our heads. This is not a divine command, but it is a beneficial practice that flows from scriptural practice. When the Lord proclaimed His name to Moses on Mount Sinai, Moses bowed his head and prostrated himself (Exodus 34:8). When Solomon prayed at the dedication of the temple as the place where the Lord had promised that His name would dwell, he knelt before the Lord (1 Kings 8:54). Jesus has received the name that is above all names, and on the Last Day every knee shall bow before Him and confess His holy name (Philippians 2:9–10).

> The Lord's name is holy; we are called to treat it accordingly.

It may seem a small gesture. To some it will appear antiquated. It is not commanded. Yet bowing the head at the mention of the holy name of the Lord teaches us to regard His name as it truly is. We teach small children to say "I'm sorry" even when they do not have a sense of sorrow so that by saying "I'm sorry" they learn that they should be sorry. So we ever teach ourselves to honor the holy name of the LORD by bowing the head at the mention of His holy name.

— Honoring My Neighbor's Name —

The LORD calls us to confess His name as above all names. He also calls us to honor the name of others. He tells us to bear no false witness against our neighbor, for that would tear down our neighbor's good name and reputation. Even speaking the truth about my neighbor for the purpose of harming his or her name is sinful. This is not the only means by which we dishonor the neighbor's name.

Names bespeak our personhood and very existence. When we refuse to speak someone's name in order to insult and demonstrate our anger with that person, we are doing far more than that, since rejecting one's name is a rejection of his or her personhood and even existence. To name something or someone is to acknowledge its existence (Ecclesiastes 6:10a); to refuse to speak someone's name is to deny that person's existence. Existence beyond this life includes the survival of your name that lives on (Ruth 4:10; Joshua 7:9). Thus, to cut off someone's name is to cut off that person's existence.

In judgment, the LORD cuts off the name of Amalek (Exodus 17:14). He promises to remove the names of those who oppose His people (Deuteronomy 7:24). He is rightly incensed at Israel because of their idolatry of the golden calf, and so He threatens to cut off their name (Deuteronomy 9:14). Saul asks David that he not cut off his name (1 Samuel 24:21). When Absalom wrests the throne from his father, David, a woman asks Absalom to preserve

> **Names bespeak our personhood and very existence.**

her husband's name (2 Samuel 14:7). One of Job's friends, Bildad, states that when the memory of a man perishes, he has no name (Job 18:17). To be nameless is to be without identity (Job 30:8). The enemies of Israel sought to wipe them out so that their name would not be remembered (Psalm 83:4). The Lord speaks judgment against Babylon, declaring that He will cut off Babylon's name (Isaiah 14:22). The Lord speaks judgment against idolatrous priests, that their names will be blotted out (Zephaniah 1:4).

While cutting off the name can be the result of just judgment, it also happens for false reasons. Jesus says that your name will be spurned as evil on His account (Luke 6:22). When your name is maligned for the sake of Christ, His name is honored. Placing Him as of higher value than the honor of the world magnifies His name as the greatest good. This is why the apostles rejoiced that they were counted worthy of suffering for the sake of His name (Acts 5:41).

With such weight being found in our names and the names of our neighbors, we are to handle one another's names with sober judgment. Refusing to speak another's name is not a light thing as it is a rejection of the very existence of a person, a person created by God and redeemed by Christ. And what of the Lord's judgment that cuts off the name? Should we fear that He would do such to us? That fear is justified when we look upon what our sin rightly merits for us. But when we look upon and trust in the promises of God in Christ, then we live in confidence. Instead of cutting off our name, Jesus becomes sin for us on the cross, being cut off by His Father, so that the Lord promises to establish our name. How great it is that God promises that His people's name shall remain (Isaiah 56:5; 66:22), which is a pledge that we shall never perish. After all, we bear His name.

The Lord delights to proclaim that He has given us a name. When the Lord calls Abram to be the line through which the

Savior would come, He promises that He will make his name great (Genesis 12:2). Moses promises God's people of old that He will establish their name (Deuteronomy 26:19). The LORD gives David success so that his name is established (1 Samuel 18:30). When Solomon ascends to the throne, the king's servants bless him, beseeching the LORD to establish his name (1 Kings 1:47). The LORD's manifold blessings upon His people cause their name to go forth among the nations as beautiful (Ezekiel 16:14). The LORD promises to restore His people so that they

> **The LORD delights to proclaim that He has given us a name.**

are named among the nations (Zephaniah 3:19). As Jerusalem faces judgment, the LORD promises that restoration shall come that will once again grant them a name (Jeremiah 33:9).

A good name is greater than riches (Proverbs 22:1; Ecclesiastes 7:1). And you have the best of names! In Baptism, you were given the name of the LORD. You are His. He honors His name by forgiving and restoring you. You bear a name that lasts into eternity.

Study Questions

1. Why does the LORD act for His name's sake? When do you act for your name's sake? When is your motivation impure?

2. Why did Israel regularly recall what the LORD did in the exodus? What do you regularly recall?

3. Discuss the tension between being called by the name of the LORD and the world beckoning you to mimic its values.

4. How does the LORD vindicate His name?

5. What does it mean that the LORD is jealous?

6. The Large Catechism teaches that "God's name is profaned when people preach, teach, and say in God's name what is false and misleading. They use His name like an ornament and attract a market for falsehood. That is, indeed, the greatest way to profane and dishonor the divine name." Where do you see this happening today?

7. How do we dishonor our neighbor's name? Instead, what ought we do?

In the Name of the Name of the Lord: Authoritative Use of the Name

"The sink is backing up again. This is really getting old."

"Okay, I will grab my tools and see what I can do."

"Why? How many times have you tried to fix this, and we end up in the same place? And each time it only gets worse. It's time to call a plumber who can fix this once and for all."

"Do you realize what that will cost? Let me have another run at it."

"Do you realize that we should have called a plumber the first time this happened? I don't want to see or smell this again. I'm calling a plumber."

"In the name of all things holy, just let me do it!"

I nvoking the name of a higher authority will grant confidence only if that higher authority has authorized you to do so. Acting in the name of another means you are acting in that person's stead so that the word you speak is not your own word but that person's. Authorization to speak in the name of another cannot be claimed; it must be given by the higher authority. And that authorization has limits. It extends only as far as the person has been authorized. The board of directors for a company may authorize an employee to execute a specific contract, but that authority extends only that far. The employee does not have authority to hire or fire other employees unless that authority has been granted separately. Likewise, the vicar ("one who stands in the place of another") only has as much authority as his bishop assigns him. The same is true for those who would speak in the name of the LORD. To speak in the name of the LORD is to speak as if your words are His. To speak in the name of the LORD is not something to be done lightly. The authority to speak in His name can be given only by Him. The authority to speak in His name goes only as far as He has authorized you to speak, no further.

— Commissioned with Authority —

S cripture is filled with incidents where the LORD commissions someone to act or speak in His name. When David arrives on the battlefield and stands before Goliath, the expectation is that the battle will be quick and that David will not survive. The battle is quick, but the victor is not as expected. David's words to Goliath reveal why the young shepherd is victorious: "You come to me with a sword and with a spear and with a javelin, but I come to you in the name of the LORD of hosts, the God of the armies of Israel, whom you have defied" (1 Samuel 17:45).

In the name of the LORD of hosts, David wields the authority of the LORD, against which Goliath cannot stand.

The prophet Elijah also acts in the name of the LORD. Unfaithful King Ahab and his wife Jezebel have been bankrolling the priests of Baal. According to Canaanite religion, Baal was the god of the sky who controlled the rain. Since Israel had chosen to depend upon Baal for rain, the LORD tells them through Elijah that He will send no rain so they can see how much rain Baal will provide. A drought ensues, lasting more than three years. Still, Israel does not repent. That their eyes might be opened to see that the LORD alone is God, Elijah confronts the prophets of Baal on Mount Carmel. There the prophets of Baal build an altar to their god, and Elijah builds "an altar in the name of the LORD" (1 Kings 18:32). The sacrifice Elijah will offer there and the words he will speak there are in the stead and by the authority of the LORD. The prophets of Baal are unable to rouse Baal to action; he does not send forth fire to consume their sacrifice as they call upon him to do. The LORD, on the other hand, responds to Elijah, who prays by His authority. Fire comes from the heavens (likely lightning, which would have been poignant since Baal was thought to control lightning as the god of the sky). Israel repents and confesses that the LORD is God. Elijah looks and sees a rain cloud on the horizon. The drought will come to an end.

Both David and Elijah act and speak faithfully in the name of the LORD. Cyrus also acts in the name of the LORD. Cyrus rose to the Persian throne in the latter half of the sixth century BC. Persia had displaced Babylon as the preeminent power. Cyrus chooses to allow the people of Judah who had been exiled during

> To speak in the name of the LORD is to speak as if your words are His.

the days of the Babylonian king Nebuchadnezzar to return home. Two centuries before Cyrus made that decision, the prophet Isaiah said he would do it. Isaiah proclaimed that the Lord had chosen Cyrus as His instrument. Though Cyrus does not know the Lord or trust in Him, he is the Lord's instrument because the Lord has called him by name: "I call you by your name, I name you, though you do not know Me" (Isaiah 45:4). Though Cyrus does not call on the name of the Lord in the same way David and Elijah do, the Lord calls Cyrus by name, bespeaking His authority over Cyrus so that Cyrus acts on His behalf to accomplish His purposes by His authority. And so Judah is freed to go home.

The Lord binds up His authority within His name. While David, Elijah, and even Cyrus are fit reminders of the good the Lord accomplishes by the authority of His name, He also teaches us that He will not tolerate the misuse of His name. "Behold, I have sworn by My great name, says the Lord, that My name shall no more be invoked by the mouth of any man of Judah in all the land of Egypt, saying, 'As the Lord God lives'" (Jeremiah 44:26). Two significant lessons come forth. First, the Lord reveals the weight and authority of His name so that when He wants to bind Himself completely, He swears by His own name. That makes sense, for His name bears the highest authority. The second lesson is that the Lord will not allow His name and the authority within His name to be abused. Since His people rejected His Word delivered by Jeremiah, He proclaims that they will not be able to invoke—that is, call upon the authority of—His name.

This should not have surprised the Lord's people. He had given warning long ago through Moses: "The prophet who presumes to speak a word in My name that I have not commanded him to speak, or who speaks in the name of other gods, that same prophet shall die" (Deuteronomy 18:20). The Lord takes seriously the right to speak in His name. The one who presumes to speak in the name of the LORD falsely is worthy of death. The lesson is quite simple. Though you will not find the practice of stoning false prophets in the Church today, those who speak on behalf of God—in the name of the LORD—shall pay heed: Don't put words into God's mouth. Only speak in His name what the LORD has given you to speak.

The sixth century BC saw the importance of this truth. The faithful prophets of the LORD had been calling His people to repentance for generations, warning them that should they not repent, they would suffer the consequence of their sin. As the day is drawing near that the LORD would act upon those warnings by sending the Babylonians to destroy Jerusalem, level the temple, and carry His people into exile, Jeremiah steps forth in the train of faithful prophets. He continues the call to repentance. And the people continue to ignore that call. They ignore the call to repentance in significant part due to the words of the false prophets. While Jeremiah stands as a solitary voice of truth, many false prophets step forth to tell people what they want to hear. Thus, Jeremiah speaks:

> **The LORD binds up His authority within His name.**

> The LORD said to me: "The prophets are prophesying lies in My name. I did not send them, nor did I command them or speak to them. They are prophesying to you a lying vision, worthless divination, and the deceit of their own minds. Therefore thus says the LORD concerning the prophets who prophesy in My name although I did not send them, and who say, 'Sword and famine shall

not come upon this land': By sword and famine those
prophets shall be consumed.'"

(Jeremiah 14:14–15)

The false prophets will pay the price for speaking falsely in
the name of the LORD. Their guilt is twofold. First, they have
dishonored the name of the LORD by claiming that they are
speaking in His name and by His authority when they are only
speaking the deceit of their own minds. Second, they have led
the people down a path of destruction. They are responsible not
only for their own fall but also for the fall of those who listened
to their lies.

This remains true today. James speaks sobering words to pastors
who are called to speak in the name of the LORD: "Not many
of you should become teachers, my brothers, for you know that
we who teach will be judged with greater strictness" (James 3:1).
The Letter to the Hebrews gives similar counsel, as pastors are
described as those who "will have to give an account" (Hebrews
13:17). St. Paul also warns young Pastor Timothy, "Keep a close
watch on yourself and on the teaching. Persist in this, for by so
doing you will save both yourself and your hearers" (1 Timothy
4:16). This is also why Paul tells the Galatians, "Even if we or
an angel from heaven should preach to you a gospel contrary
to the one we preached to you, let him be accursed" (Galatians
1:8). Even more sobering are Paul's words to the Romans about
those who teach contrary to the Word of God: "Though they
know God's righteous decree that those who practice such things
deserve to die, they not only do them but give approval to those
who practice them" (Romans 1:32).

The lesson is simple yet profound. Pastors and anyone else
who would speak in the name of the LORD will give an account
to Christ for what was spoken in His name. Therefore, wisely

choose your words. Do not speak in the name of the LORD what He has not Himself given you to say in His Word.

The lesson for others is similar. Weigh the word of pastors against God's Word. If what they say is not found in Scripture, they are not speaking by Christ's authority. Whether it be your pastor from the pulpit or Bible study, a television personality with a huge congregation and broadcast audience, or a best-selling author, weigh what is said against Scripture. The pastor who departs from the clear Word of God has forfeited his right to be heeded.

— Jesus Comes in the Name of the LORD —

You need never doubt whether Christ truly speaks in the name of the LORD. He enters Jerusalem to cries of "Blessed is He who comes in the name of the Lord!" (Matthew 21:9). The crowds rightly confess that Jesus comes in the name of the LORD, that is, with divine authority. This is His prophetic office. He delivers the Word of the LORD. Indeed, He is the Prophet of prophets because He goes about delivering the Word of the LORD as no one else ever has or ever will. He is the LORD in the midst of His people, delivering His Word to them. While the prophets would appeal to the highest authority by saying, "Thus says the Lord," Jesus never uses that phrase. Instead, He appeals to the highest authority by saying, "I say to you" (Matthew 5:22, 28, 32, 34, 39, 44). Jesus appeals to Himself as the highest authority. The crowds who listen to Him realize this and marvel at Him because He teaches as one with authority (Matthew 7:28–29).

Christians take hold of Christ's authority when they speak in His name. But His name is not a magic formula by which you can claim what you desire to teach. To speak in His name is to submit to His authority. Submission is about order. Submission to

His authority means you speak what He has given you to speak, following the order He has established rather than creating your own order that would put words in His mouth. Even those who claim to speak in the name of Christ are not speaking in His name and by His authority unless their words flow from Christ's own words given to us in Scripture. Jesus makes this clear:

> "Not everyone who says to Me, 'Lord, Lord,' will enter the kingdom of heaven, but the one who does the will of My Father who is in heaven. On that day many will say to Me, 'Lord, Lord, did we not prophesy in Your name, and cast out demons in Your name, and do many mighty works in Your name?' And then I will declare to them, 'I never knew you; depart from Me, you workers of lawlessness.'"
>
> *(Matthew 7:21–23)*

The Sermon on the Mount presents a great deal of comfort, such as Christ's teaching that we need not fear for tomorrow because He provides for us abundantly (Matthew 6:25–34). There is also plenty to challenge us in the Sermon on the Mount, including the sobering words that not all who prophesy, cast out demons, and do mighty works in Christ's name are acting by His authority. This is yet another reminder to weigh the words of all who claim to be speaking in Christ's name, holding them up against Scripture. Have they submitted themselves to the authority of Christ in His Word, or have they sought to use His name as a tool to accomplish their own ends? Faith trusts in Christ so that we

> **Christians take hold of Christ's authority when they speak in His name.**

follow His direction rather than believe that we can dictate to Him what ought to be done.

Jesus also teaches us to rejoice when others faithfully act in His name. "John said to Him, 'Teacher, we saw someone casting out demons in Your name, and we tried to stop him, because he was not following us.' But Jesus said, 'Do not stop him, for no one who does a mighty work in My name will be able soon afterward to speak evil of Me'" (Mark 9:38–39). John was concerned whether this person in question was following the disciples. Jesus redirects the focus away from them to whether the person is acting by faith in Christ. This underscores the criteria for weighing the words of those who claim to act in the name of Christ. It is not a question of whether they follow us but whether their words and actions are submissive to the authority of Christ in His Word.

The name of Jesus bears all authority but only for those who trust in Him. Those who neither trust Him nor submit to His authority do not speak in His name. In other words, to act and speak in the name of Jesus is to act and speak according to His will, not our own. He reveals His will to us specifically in Scripture. Those who speak and act by His authority conform themselves to Scripture.

But those who do submit to Christ's authority act mightily. As He sends out the Twelve, Jesus says, "Whoever receives you receives Me, and whoever receives Me receives Him who sent Me" (Matthew 10:40). Christ acts by the Father's authority. He entrusts that authority to His apostles, who are sent in His name. So He promises us, "If you ask Me anything in My name, I will do it" (John 14:14). Again, this is not Christ offering His name as a magic formula by which you can garner whatever you desire. Here Christ promises that He will grant whatever you ask by His authority, which is revealed in His Word. You can have confidence when you ask in His name for what He has promised, such as the forgiveness of your sin. You can have confidence when you ask for things such as physical healing, which He has promised will be fully given in life everlasting, though it may not come in this life. You cannot have confidence when you ask for what He has not promised, such as financial riches. He has promised that your riches are an eternal inheritance that exceed gold and silver, purchased only by His blood.

— The Acts of the Apostles — in the Name of Jesus

The Book of Acts is replete with accounts of the apostles acting in the name of Jesus. Their authoritative use of Christ's name sets up the authoritative use of His name in the life of the Church.

As they are nearing the temple, Peter and John happen upon a lame beggar who asks for alms. Being without money to give the man in need, Peter says to him, "In the name of Jesus Christ of Nazareth, rise up and walk!" (Acts 3:6). By the authority of Christ, the man does that very thing. This creates quite a stir, so Peter and John are surrounded by a crowd. Peter testifies to them of the death and resurrection of Christ. Peter continues, "And His name—by faith in His name—has made this man strong whom you seek and know, and the faith that is through Jesus has given the man this perfect health in the presence of you all" (Acts 3:16). Peter makes clear that the authority of Christ can only be taken hold of by faith. And faith takes hold of a clear promise of God.

Peter and John are subsequently arrested and then questioned: "By what power or by what name did you do this?" (Acts 4:7). Peter replies, "Let it be known to all of you and to all the people of Israel that by the name of Jesus Christ of Nazareth, whom you crucified, whom God raised from the dead—by Him this man is standing before you well" (Acts 4:10). Peter continues to proclaim and act in the name of Christ, by His authority. The result is that they charged Peter and John "not to speak or teach at all in the name of Jesus" (Acts 4:18). Those who

> **The authority of Christ can only be taken hold of by faith.**

arrested and questioned Peter and John rejected the authority of Jesus; they rejected His name. Peter and John upheld Jesus' name and authority.

Peter and John are not alone in acting in the name of Jesus. Philip does so while preaching in Samaria. "When they believed Philip as he preached good news about the kingdom of God and the name of Jesus Christ, they were baptized, both men and women" (Acts 8:12). The name of Jesus—His authority—is specifically tied to Baptism. That pattern continues throughout the Book of Acts, where there is repeated reference to the newly converted being baptized in the name of Jesus. This is not contrary to Jesus' institution of Baptism in the name of the Father and of the Son and of Holy Spirit (Matthew 28:19). While Matthew records the institution of Baptism in the name of the Trinity, the Book of Acts focuses upon the authority of Christ and thus speaks of Baptism being done in His name.

The name of Christ again comes center stage in the conversion of Saul (who later takes on the name Paul). Christ appears to Saul when he is traveling to Damascus. Having been blinded by the light of Christ, Saul waits in Damascus three days until the Lord sends to him Ananias. Knowing Saul's reputation as a persecutor of Christ's Church, Ananias is reluctant. The Lord tells him that Saul "is a chosen instrument of Mine to carry My name before the Gentiles and kings and the children of Israel.

For I will show him how much he must suffer for the sake of My name" (Acts 9:15–16). Saul not only will carry Christ's name, and therefore His authority to forgive and save the Gentiles, but will also suffer for Christ's name.

By the time of his third missionary journey, Saul is known as Paul and travels to Ephesus. Scripture tells us:

> And God was doing extraordinary miracles by the hands of Paul, so that even handkerchiefs or aprons that had touched his skin were carried away to the sick, and their diseases left them and the evil spirits came out of them. Then some of the itinerant Jewish exorcists undertook to invoke the name of the Lord Jesus over those who had evil spirits, saying, "I adjure you by the Jesus whom Paul proclaims." Seven sons of a Jewish high priest named Sceva were doing this. But the evil spirit answered them, "Jesus I know, and Paul I recognize, but who are you?" And the man in whom was the evil spirit leaped on them, mastered all of them and overpowered them, so that they fled out of that house naked and wounded. And this became known to all the residents of Ephesus, both Jews and Greeks. And fear fell upon them all, and the name of the Lord Jesus was extolled. Also many of those who were now believers came, confessing and divulging their practices. And a number of those who had practiced magic arts brought their books together and burned them in the sight of all. And they counted the value of them and found it came to fifty thousand pieces of silver. So the word of the Lord continued to increase and prevail mightily.
>
> *(Acts 19:11–20)*

Two key lessons emerge from this incident. First, Christ will not suffer His name to be manipulated by others. When those who are without faith in Christ seek to use His name to their own ends, the results are not favorable for them. Even if they are seeking noble ends, it does not go well, because Christ's name is being used as a tool rather than being honored as His to give and use as He desires. The evil spirits must submit to Christ's authority, and so they had to submit to Paul, who acted under Christ's authority. But those who used Christ's name as a magic formula to their own ends found the evil spirits to be overpowering because they were not acting under Christ's authority.

The second lesson is that the name of Christ is extolled. Even though the crowds marvel at Paul's actions so that they long for handkerchiefs and napkins he had touched, it is not Paul's name that is extolled. Paul makes it clear that it is not by his own name and authority that these mighty works are being done. It is only by the authority of Christ. It is His name that is extolled.

Why don't we see such miraculous healings today? There are incidents when medical staff state that they have done everything they can and that the family should prepare for their loved one's death, only to have the patient recover. The LORD still heals today—often through the medical sciences, but also miraculously.

Evil spirits are also cast out today. While it can happen in any setting, missionaries tell incredible stories.

So why have I never had anyone seeking my handkerchief, believing it could heal them? There is a distinction between the pastoral office and the apostolic office. The apostles carried an authority that pastors do not.

The qualifications for being an apostle included being an eyewitness of the resurrected Christ, something that pastors cannot claim. Thus, the apostles were sent by Christ immediately. Pastors, on other hand, are sent by Christ mediately, that is, by His chosen means. Pastors are sent by Christ through the Church, which calls men into the pastoral office. Being mediately called, pastors cannot act or speak with the same authority as the apostles. Pastors teach and act authoritatively as they submit to the clear Word of God. Apostles, on the other hand, were the Lord's chosen means to speak that clear Word of God that is now recorded for us in the New Testament.

We confess in the Nicene Creed that we believe in one holy Christian and apostolic Church. We confess that we hold to the same faith as the apostles, the faith that has been handed on to us by Christ through those apostles. The Father sent forth the Son in His name. The Son sent the apostles in His name. The apostles hand on the authority of Christ to the Church, an authority that submits to Christ as revealed in Scripture, an authority that pastors utilize as they faithfully speak what Christ has given through the apostles.

Beware those who claim to be apostles today. That is a claim to authority that has not been given to them. It is a claim to authority to establish doctrine, as Peter, James, John, Paul, and the rest of the apostolic band established through their writings that proclaimed who Christ is and what He has done for us. The authority of the Church today is not found in proclaiming new doctrine but in extolling the name of Christ—His name and authority given to us in Scripture.

Study Questions

1. To speak in the name of the LORD is to speak as if your words are His. It is a serious thing to speak in His name. What might tempt you to overstep and claim to speak in His name what He has not authorized you to speak?

2. Why does the LORD swear by His own name?

3. What was the twofold guilt of the false prophets in the days of Jeremiah? Which do find to be the graver type of guilt?

4. Whose words do you need to weigh against Scripture?

5. What do we mean when we say that Jesus is the Prophet of prophets?

6. "To act and speak in the name of Jesus is to act and speak according to His will, not our own." How can you know if you are speaking according to His will?

7. What does it mean in the Book of Acts that the apostles baptized in the name of Jesus?

O Jesus Christ: The Name of the Lord Fulfilled in Jesus

"I keep looking this over and the figures are not accurate. I don't know whether to think that you were rushing through this and made a lot of mistakes, if you don't understand how to complete this properly, if you don't care, or if you're trying to hide something."

"Are you still going on about that? You're making a mountain out of a molehill."

"This is not a molehill. Regulations are in place for a reason, and if we don't honor them, we jeopardize this company and everything we've worked to build."

"You need to lighten up."

"No, you need to take this seriously. Do it right."

"Oh J**** C*****!"

Using the name of Christ as an expletive is provocative because of who He is. Since His personal name is being used in vain, I cannot bring myself to type it out in this illustration. The names of other religious figures are not drained of their meaning and then reused as an obscenity, because their names do not carry the same weight. Jesus comes forth as God in human flesh, making His name to be the very name of God.

Everything that the LORD packs into His name is found in Christ. In the name of Jesus, the LORD dwells among us. In the name of Jesus, the LORD's being resides. In the name of Jesus, the LORD acts with authority. In the name of Jesus, the LORD claims us as His own. In the name of Jesus is all the fullness of the LORD.

— Christ Prophesied as the Fulfillment — of the Name of the LORD

That the LORD would dwell in Christ and His name is promised in the words of Solomon as he prays at the dedication of the temple: "Now the LORD has fulfilled His promise that He made. For I have risen in the place of David my father, and sit on the throne of Israel, as the LORD promised, and I have built the house for the name of the LORD, the God of Israel" (1 Kings 8:20). Solomon is the son of David who the LORD promised would build the temple where He would dwell among His people. Four centuries after Solomon, the temple would lie in ruins, but that does not mean that the LORD's promise was broken. He sent forth the greater Son of David in Christ, who would become the temple Himself.

> Everything that the LORD packs into His name is found in Christ.

Jesus bears the title "son of David" (Matthew 1:1) not only because He is descended from David's line but also because He is the fulfillment of the messianic prophecies about the Son the David. The promise that the Son of David would build the temple was fulfilled in part through Solomon. The promise comes to its fullness in Jesus Christ, the Son of David, who is the temple.

So we learn in John 2:19–22, where Jesus says, "Destroy this temple, and in three days I will raise it." His point is lost on those who hear Him speak this. It would not be until after His resurrection that His disciples would understand that He was not referring to the physical building at which they marveled but to the temple of His body. Jesus' point is simple yet profound. He is the temple. He is the locale where the Lord dwells among His people. As the name of the Lord dwelt in the temple, now His name dwells in Christ. Do not look for the Lord outside of Christ, for He will not be found outside His name.

The same is taught in Psalm 22. The words of verse 1 are on Jesus' lips at the cross with the cry of dereliction, "My God, My God, why have You forsaken Me?" Those words capture the depth of Christ's suffering as He is abandoned by His Father, bearing the Father's wrath against the sin of the world. In an oral culture like the one in which Christ lived, the quotation of a single verse would prompt remembrance of the entirety of a psalm. That is quite appropriate in this instance as there is much of Psalm 22 that finds its fulfillment in Christ's crucifixion. Verses 6–8 describe the mockery to which Jesus is subjected on the cross. The circling of His enemies around Him is captured in verses 12–13. Christ's physical suffering is given specific attention in verses 14–15. The Roman soldiers are described as "dogs" (a biblical means of referring to unbelievers, since dogs were unclean by the standards of biblical cleanliness) who divide Christ's garments and cast lots for His clothes (vv. 16–18). Yet, amid all this, Christ remains steadfast in His trust in His Father (vv. 19–20). Most poignant for this study is Psalm 22:22: "I will tell of Your name to My brothers." The promise all along has been that the Savior who would fulfill Psalm 22 would tell of the name of the LORD to His brothers. He reveals that name to His disciples, to us, to all, by fulfilling that name. He is the LORD's dwelling among us by fulfilling His name.

— Jesus and His Name — Cannot Be Separated

Just as the LORD cannot be separated from His name—where His name is, He is, and what is done to His name is done to Him—so it is also with the name of Jesus. This is especially seen in the writings of the apostle John. This usage is driven by the conventions of Hebrew that are found throughout the Old Testament and are brought into the New Testament by John and others who were trained in the Scriptures. In the opening account of his Gospel, John speaks of the faithful as those "who did receive Him, who believed in His name" (John 1:12). Notice the parallel between Jesus and His name. To receive Jesus is to believe in His name. What is done to Jesus' name is done to Him.

The union between Jesus and His name continues in the next chapter, as "many believed in His name when they saw the signs that He was doing" (John 2:23). Faith in Jesus' name is the same as faith in Jesus because He and His name are inseparable. Faith in the name of Jesus is again brought forth in John 3:18: "Whoever believes in Him is not condemned, but whoever does not believe is condemned already, because he has not believed in the name of the only Son of God." John takes up this same teaching in his first epistle as he says God's command is that we "believe in the name of His Son Jesus Christ" (1 John 3:23).

Later in the epistle, John says, "I write these things to you who believe in the name of the Son of God, that you may know that you have eternal life" (1 John 5:13). These passages from 1 John echo what he wrote in John 20:31: "These are written so that you may believe that Jesus is the Christ, the Son of God, and that by believing you may have life in His name." Not only is there the ongoing teaching of faith in the name of Jesus, but His name is also paralleled with His identity as Christ, the Son of God.

While John gives attention to the unity between Jesus and His name, the same is taught elsewhere. Matthew records these words of Jesus: "Everyone who has left houses or brothers or sisters or father or mother or children or lands, for My name's sake, will receive a hundredfold and will inherit eternal life" (Matthew 19:29). Jesus speaks of the cost of following Him that includes leaving house and family for His name's sake. To leave for the sake of His name is to leave for His sake. There is a parallel passage to this in Mark 10:29–30: "There is no one who has left house or brothers or sisters or mother or father or children or lands, for My sake and for the gospel, who will not receive a hundredfold now in this time, houses and brothers and sisters and mothers and children and lands, with persecutions, and in the age to come eternal life." Again, to leave for His name's sake is to leave for the sake of Jesus Himself. Jesus' words here also give focus to what is bound up in Jesus' name—the Gospel. When you have the name of Jesus, you have the Good News of the Lord's salvation.

> **To receive Jesus is to believe in His name.**

The apostles were well taught by Christ so that their actions and teaching in the Book of Acts follow this pattern. Having been beaten because of their proclamation of the name of Jesus, the apostles "left the presence of the council, rejoicing that they were counted worthy to suffer dishonor for the name" (Acts 5:41). The weight of Christ's name is evident as the shorthand "the name" is used. That would be an expected shorthand for the name of the LORD, which it is. But it is also used as shorthand for the name of Jesus, as His name and the name of the LORD are one and the same.

As he stands before Agrippa, the apostle Paul also teaches the inseparability of Jesus from His name: "I myself was convinced that I ought to do many things in opposing the name of Jesus of Nazareth" (Acts 26:9). Paul knows that his former ways of opposing the name of Jesus constituted opposition to Jesus Himself. Having repented of that opposition, he proclaims the name of Jesus.

— The Name of Jesus Cannot Be Separated — from the Name of the LORD

"The name" is shorthand both for the name of the LORD and for the name of Jesus in Acts 5:41 because they are one and the same. This is taught throughout the New Testament. The name of Jesus and the name of the LORD are inseparable. It is the teaching of the apostle John: "The Jews gathered around Him and said to Him, 'How long will You keep us in suspense? If You are the Christ, tell us plainly.' Jesus answered them, 'I told you, and you do not believe. The works that I do in My Father's name bear witness about Me'" (John 10:24–25). Jesus' acts are done in the Father's name because He does them by the Father's authority. Christ acts with the Father's authority because His name and the Father's name are bound together. This comes forth again in John 5:43, where Jesus says, "I have come in My Father's name, and you do not receive Me." Jesus' actions are the

Father's actions because there is no separating Jesus' name from the name of the Lord.

Matthew joins John in delivering this teaching of Jesus. As the time of His suffering and death draws near, Jesus laments over Jerusalem, looking toward the Last Day. He is sorrowful over their persistent rejection of those sent to them. They rejected the prophets of old; they rejected John the Baptist; now, they reject Jesus. Their rejection fuels His lamentation for the present time but even more for the Last Day, when judgment for such sin will not be avoided. Jesus cries, "I tell you, you will not see Me again, until you say, 'Blessed is He who comes in the name of the Lord'" (Matthew 23:39). That was the acclamation at His triumphal entry into Jerusalem just days earlier. It will also be proclaimed aloud at His return. The Last Day is regularly described as "the Day of the Lord" throughout the Prophets. Jesus lays claim to that day as being of His name, equating His name with the name of the Lord.

> The name of Jesus and the name of the Lord are inseparable.

Because Jesus' name and the name of the Lord cannot be separated, His people put Jesus' name in place of the name of the Lord. It happens in the title that believers gladly take upon themselves in the Book of Acts: "In Antioch the disciples were first called Christians" (Acts 11:26). The title "Christian" makes sense for believers because it speaks to the source of our salvation—it is found only in Christ. It also bespeaks our identity as belonging to Christ. To say that we belong to Christ is to equate Him with the Lord. He calls the faithful "My people who are called by My name" (2 Chronicles 7:14). We are called by the name of the Lord, which is to say we are called by the name of Christ. We are Christians.

This is in concert with the teaching of John mentioned earlier. "To all who did receive Him, who believed in His name, He gave the right to become children of God, who were born, not of blood nor of the will of the flesh nor of the will of man, but of God" (John 1:12–13). Faith is born from divine initiative. Faith is not the result of human will but of God. This puts John's later teaching in proper perspective: "This is His commandment, that we believe in the name of His Son Jesus Christ" (1 John 3:23). Faith is not the result of obedience to God's command, because that would place faith in the realm of human decision. Instead, God's command causes faith to be born in us.

Because faith is born of God rather than human will, we see again that the name of Jesus cannot be separated from the name of the LORD. John speaks of the faithful as having "believed in His name" (John 1:12; 2:23). This belief in the name of Jesus builds on the teaching of such texts as Psalm 33:21: "Our heart is glad in Him, because we trust in His holy name." The context is clear that it is in the holy name of the LORD that we trust. Isaiah speaks similarly: "Let him who walks in darkness and has no light trust in the name of the LORD and rely on his God" (Isaiah 50:10). The LORD is the object of faith. John does not blush when he calls us to believe in the name of Jesus, since His name is the fulfillment of the name of the LORD.

The apostle Paul also places priority upon the name of Jesus and its union with the name of the LORD. Before his conversion, Paul was known for persecuting those who called on the name of Jesus (Acts 9:14, 21), the same usage of the name of Jesus that places it in parallel with the name of the LORD. While Acts reports this about Paul, he chooses to use that same language when he addresses the Corinthians and numbers them among "all those who in every place call upon the name of our Lord Jesus Christ" (1 Corinthians 1:2).

Peter does much the same thing. Peter delivers his Pentecost sermon, quoting from Joel 2, and says, "It shall come to pass that everyone who calls upon the name of the Lord shall be saved" (Acts 2:21). While the Book of Acts does not make it clear, the quotation from Joel uses the personal name of God, Yahweh. All who call on the name of the Lord will be saved. Then Peter calls upon his hearers to be baptized in the name of Jesus for their salvation (Acts 2:38). The name of Jesus and the name of the Lord are interchangeable in Peter's preaching.

This also underscores the trinitarian nature of the Lord. When Peter calls upon his hearers to be baptized in the name of Jesus, he also speaks of the promised Holy Spirit (Acts 2:38). Yet Peter also speaks of calling on the Father (1 Peter 1:17). The Father, Son, and Holy Spirit are bound together as you call upon the name of the Lord. To call on the name of Jesus is to call on the Father and the Spirit, all three together. To call upon the name of Jesus is to call on the name of the Lord because it is upon His name that the faithful call. "Abram called upon the name of the Lord" (Genesis 13:4). "Oh give thanks to the Lord; call upon His name" (Psalm 105:1).

— The Name of Jesus Reveals the Lord —

The name of the Lord is a theophany; it reveals Him to us that we might know Him (see the chapter entitled "With God as My Witness: The Name of the Lord Delivering His Presence"). Since the name of Jesus and the name of the Lord are interchangeable, it is not surprising that the name of Jesus reveals the Lord to us. On the night He is betrayed, Jesus prays to the Father, offering a prayer that recalls what He has accomplished: "I have manifested Your name to the people whom You gave me out of the world. . . . I made known to them Your name, and

I will continue to make it known, that the love with which You have loved Me may be in them, and I in them" (John 17:6, 26). Jesus reveals the LORD by revealing His name. And Jesus alone can do that. To know Jesus is to know the Father (John 14:7). To see Jesus is to see the Father (John 14:9). No one has seen the Father, yet Jesus makes Him known (John 1:18). Jesus does that by revealing the Father's name, the name of the LORD.

Jesus displays His divine Sonship by revealing the name of the LORD. Only the Son can lay claim to revealing the name of the LORD. The revelation of the Father's name is Christ's highest work. And look what He reveals of God! In Christ you receive the revelation of the LORD's grace and mercy.

Just as Jesus reveals the Father by His name, so also only the Father can name Jesus, as it is an act of authority. The Father not only names Jesus, but He then uses Jesus' name to reveal who He is to Joseph (Matthew 1:21). An angel of the Lord tells Joseph that the name given to the child born of Mary shall be *Jesus* because He will save His people from their sins. The name is *Yeshua* (Hebrew for "Yahweh is salvation"), which is brought into English as Joshua. But we are accustomed to saying Jesus due to the phonetic changes resulting from the transition from Hebrew to Greek to English. Aside from matters of pronunciation, the name of Jesus is given by the Father that His identity might be revealed to us. He is the one who saves us. And since His name means "Yahweh is salvation," the Father reveals that Jesus is Yahweh, the LORD.

— Jesus—the Name of Salvation —

The name of Jesus reveals His saving work and identity. Though their understanding of how Jesus would bring about salvation was limited at that moment, the crowd on Palm

Sunday captures His saving work and identity. They are saying more than they realize. They cry out, "Blessed is He who comes in the name of the Lord!" (Mark 11:9). He comes into Jerusalem by the authority of the LORD to fulfill His name, to be "Yahweh is salvation."

Jesus' fulfillment of the name of the LORD is bound up in His cross. On Holy Thursday, with the cross looming before Him, Jesus is in anguish. He says, "Now is My soul troubled. And what shall I say? 'Father, save Me from this hour'? But for this purpose I have come to this hour. Father, glorify Your name" (John 12:27–28). Of course Jesus is in anguish. He faces not just death, not just crucifixion, but the sin of

> Jesus displays His divine Sonship by revealing the name of the LORD.

the world being given to Him. He will take on the righteous wrath of God against sin in its entirety. Yet this is the very means by which the Father's name, the name of the LORD, is glorified. At the cross, Jesus fulfills His own name, for by His suffering and death, the LORD Jesus saves His people from their sin.

The apostles trust Jesus to be who His name says He is. And so they proclaim it. When Peter and John are asked by what authority they made a lame man to walk, they do not hold back. They not only confess that it is by the authority of Jesus that they have healed the man, but also that His name is the sole means of salvation. Peter says, "There is salvation in no one else, for there is no other name under heaven given among men by which we must be saved" (Acts 4:12). Jesus, "Yahweh is salvation," fulfills His name.

The apostles were bold in their confession. What are you to do with the name of Jesus, which is the name of the LORD, and which delivers His salvation? That is the topic of the next chapter.

Study Questions

1. How is Solomon's dedication of the temple a promise of Christ?

2. What does Psalm 22 reveal about Jesus' fulfillment of the name of the LORD?

3. Where does John teach that Jesus and His name are inseparable?

4. "Jesus' actions are the Father's actions because there is no separating Jesus' name from the name of the LORD." What significance does this phrase hold for the doctrine of the Trinity?

5. Why does John not blush when he calls us to believe in the name of Jesus?

6. What is Christ's highest work?

Good Lord: The Name of the Lord in the Life of the Church

My wife was walking through the grocery store when another customer blurted out, "Good Lord!"

She replied, "He most certainly is."

The Lord is good. Many were raised to end meals praying, "Oh, give thanks to the Lord, for He is good." That is taken right from the Psalms (Psalm 136:1 is but one example). Knowing that the Lord is good, the Church has brought His name into the liturgy. From ancient times, the faithful have chanted the Kyrie (Greek vocative for "Lord!"). We chant, "Lord, have mercy. Christ, have mercy. Lord, have mercy." Those are not vain words but confident words because the Lord is good. And He delivers all His goodness to us in His name.

When the Church takes hold of the name of the LORD, we are seizing the joy of the Last Day. Yes, there is joy for Christ's people on the Last Day. Though Scripture speaks of the Last Day in ominous terms and does not refrain from describing the judgment that will come on that day, Scripture also is replete with teachings that the Last Day is to be anticipated by the faithful. The Church's prayer is "Come, Lord Jesus!" (Revelation 22:20). We long for His return because with Him will come the restoration of all things, death's destruction, and the joy of seeing the LORD face-to-face.

The joy of the Last Day is bound up in the name of the LORD. The prophet Zechariah describes the Last Day, saying, "The LORD will be king over all the earth. On that day the LORD will be one and His name one" (Zechariah 14:9). This is a promise of the fulfillment of Deuteronomy 6:4, often referred to as "The Great *Shema*" (*Shema* is Hebrew for "Hear!"). Through Moses, the LORD says, "Hear, O Israel: The LORD our God, the LORD is one." The LORD is one in that He is alone. No other is God. Right now, He alone is God, though there are many false gods that grab the attention and loyalty of humans. But on the Last Day, all those false gods will be seen for what they are and will fall away. The LORD alone will be confessed as God.

The apostle Paul seizes this eschatological (end-times) joy in the name of the LORD in his Letter to the Church in Philippi. Philippians 2:6–11 is known as the "*Carmen Christi*" (Latin for "The Song of Christ"). It is not apparent in the English translation, but in the original Greek, it is poetic in form, revealing that it was a hymn sung by first-century Christians. Verses 6–8 confess Jesus' state of humiliation, that though He remained fully divine with all divine power and authority, He chose to not utilize His full authority, so that He suffered and died for our salvation. Verses 9–11 focus upon Jesus' state of exaltation:

having earned our salvation, from His grave and into eternity, He uses His full divine authority to deliver the salvation He won for us. The resurrection of Christ overflows with His exaltation. On the Last Day, He will raise us just as He was raised. When that happens, His name will be preeminent. Paul says that at the name of Jesus every knee shall bow, and every tongue will confess that Jesus Christ is Lord, to the glory of God the Father (Philippians 2:10–11). Every knee will bow at the name of Jesus because He is the Lord. The knees and tongues of the faithful will be full of joy at that day.

This eschatological joy awaits us. But we do not need to wait for it. On the Last Day, the joy will be ours in full. Now it is ours in part. The end-times joy breaks into the present time as we receive the name of the Lord in Christ. Receiving the name of the Lord, the Church joyfully calls upon Him.

— Calling On the Name of the Lord —

Part of the Church's joyful response is to call on the name of the Lord. To be able to call on the name of the Lord, you must first know His name. And to know His name is to know Him as He has revealed Himself. Knowing the Lord as He has revealed Himself engenders faith. We trust Him because of who He is. The psalmist says, "Those who know Your name put their trust in You, for You, O Lord, have not forsaken those who seek You" (Psalm 9:10). He has revealed His name and very self in time. Yet the knowledge of His name brings us to the end times. John describes the victorious Christ coming on a white horse. The description is majestic. "His eyes are like a flame of fire, and

> On the Last Day, the name of the Lord will be preeminent.

on His head are many diadems, and He has a name written that no one knows but Himself" (Revelation 19:12). Only Christ knows the name of the LORD for He bears the name of the LORD.

Though Christ alone knows that name, He does not withhold it from us. He makes the name of the LORD known (John 17:6, 26). When He reveals the name, worship naturally results. Worship is seen as the faithful people call on the name of the LORD. The earliest generations of man called on the name of the LORD (Genesis 4:26). Faithful Abram built an altar and called on the name of the LORD (Genesis 12:8; 13:4). He would call on Him again later when he arrived at Beersheba (Genesis 21:33). Isaac also built an altar and called on the name of the LORD (Genesis 26:25). Naaman the Syrian expected faithful Elisha to call on the name of the LORD (2 Kings 5:11). The psalmist says, "We give thanks to You, O God; we give thanks, for Your name is near. We recount Your wondrous deeds" (Psalm 75:1). The Psalms also distinguish the faithful from the unfaithful by saying that those who do not know the LORD are those who do not call upon His name (Psalm 79:6). Jeremiah also says that those who do not know the LORD do not call on His name (Jeremiah 10:25). Yet, Isaiah promises that the LORD so longs to save all people that He calls out, "Here am I, here am I" to those who are not yet called by His name (Isaiah 65:1).

To call on the name of the LORD is to worship Him. It demonstrates both dependence and trust. The one calling on the name of the LORD recognizes that he does not have the answer to his trouble; he is dependent upon the LORD giving answer. Yet you do not call upon one who would likely harm you. You call upon the One who helps in time of need. Worship flows from dependence and trust.

Why can you trust the LORD? Because He has revealed His nature and character to you by His name. Packed into His name are His grace and mercy. His name delivers His salvation. His name reveals His saving work in Christ.

— Blessing the Name of the LORD —

Worship also takes place as you bless the name of the LORD. Job's children are killed, and his property is lost in short order. Satan expects Job to turn against the LORD. Instead, Job says, "Naked I came from my mother's womb, and naked shall I return. The LORD gave, and the LORD has taken away; blessed be the name of the LORD" (Job 1:21). This is Job's confession, that he trusts in the LORD despite his circumstances. Though he has lost children and possessions, he will bless the name of the LORD because what he has in the LORD is greater than what he has lost.

> To call on the name of the LORD is to worship Him.

The psalmist proclaims, "Sing to the LORD, bless His name; tell of His salvation from day to day" (Psalm 96:2). In good Hebrew poetic style, there is beautiful parallelism in this verse, as the second line unpacks the first line. How do you bless the name of the LORD? By telling of His salvation. Worship does not center upon the worshiper but upon the One who is being worshiped. There is no greater worship of the LORD than recounting His saving work and receiving the benefits of it.

David teaches the same in Psalm 103. Verse 1 states, "Bless the LORD, O my soul, and all that is within me, bless His holy name!" The parallelism equates the LORD and His name. To bless the LORD is to bless His name. To bless the name of the LORD is to bless Him. The rest of the psalm sets forth how you bless His name: namely, by recounting His saving works and receiving the benefits of what He has done. This worship is done with the whole of your being. David calls upon his soul to bless the Lord. Western thought, informed by Greek philosophy, divides body and soul, thinking of the soul as your immaterial substance that is distinct and separate from your body. Scripture has something different in mind when it speaks of your soul. Your soul is your very being, encapsulating the whole of you including your body and every other part of you. When David calls upon his soul to bless the Lord, he is calling for his whole being to worship the Lord.

Psalm 103:2–5 summarizes well how the whole of your being blesses the Lord. David repeats the call for his soul to bless the Lord and then says to not forget all His benefits. Lest His benefits be forgotten, David recites them, beginning with forgiveness:

> Bless the Lord, O my soul,
> and forget not all His benefits,
> who forgives all your iniquity,
> who heals all your diseases,
> who redeems your life from the pit,
> who crowns you with steadfast love and mercy,
> who satisfies you with good
> so that your youth is renewed like the eagle's.

— Giving Thanks to the Name of the Lord —

The worship of the Lord also takes place by giving thanks to His name. Since you cannot separate the Lord from His name, to give thanks to His name is to give thanks to Him. David again teaches us to worship the Lord. As David establishes Jerusalem as the capital of the kingdom of Israel, he has the tabernacle set up in Jerusalem. Great festivities attend the entrance of the ark into Jerusalem and the tabernacle. David offers a song of thanks to the LORD by recounting all that He has done for His people. As seen before, worship focuses on recounting the deeds of the LORD and the delivery of the benefits of His salvation to His people. David's song comes to a conclusion in 1 Chronicles 16:35–36, where David sings, "Save us, O God of our salvation, and gather and deliver us from among the nations, that we may give thanks to Your holy name and glory in Your praise. Blessed be the LORD, the God of Israel, from everlasting to everlasting!" To David's prayer all the people cry out, "Amen!" Since we cannot save ourselves, worship expresses our dependence upon and trust in the LORD to save us. The natural response to the gift of His salvation is hearty thanks to His name.

David teaches this another time, in Psalm 54. During the days when Saul was seeking David's life, David learned dependence upon the LORD. This psalm was written in that context. David is on the run from Saul, so he prays, "O God, save me by Your name, and vindicate me by Your might" (Psalm 54:1). David knows salvation is found in the name of the LORD. The psalm begins with reference to the name of the LORD, and it ends that way as well. In verses 6–7, David says, "With a freewill offering I will sacrifice to You; I will give thanks to Your name, O LORD, for it is good. For He has delivered me from every trouble, and my eye has looked in triumph on my enemies." David gives thanks to the LORD because His name is good. And David tells us in what that goodness is found. The LORD delivers David. Yet again, the focus of worship is upon the saving acts of the LORD.

— Praising the Name of the LORD —

The faithful worship the LORD also by praising His name. As Moses nears the end of his earthly life, he sings for all of Israel. Praise of the LORD is not directed to Him but to others, telling them about what He has done. Early in his song, Moses sings, "I will proclaim the name of the LORD; ascribe greatness to our God!" (Deuteronomy 32:3). Then Moses proclaims the name of the LORD by proclaiming all that He has done for His people. Moses' song is so great that it is sung by those who are victorious over the beast in Revelation 15:4.

David learned well from Moses so that he also praises the name of the LORD as his earthly life draws to a close. David's song of deliverance is recorded in 2 Samuel 22. Though it recalls how the LORD delivered him from the hand of Saul many years earlier, it is placed into the narrative flow of 2 Samuel near the end of David's life. He recounts all that the LORD has done for him. As his song nears its end, David sings, "For this I will praise You, O LORD, among the nations, and sing praises to Your name" (v. 50). This is another example where the LORD and His name are interchangeable, as both are the objects of praise in this verse. This is also another example of how the praise of the name is bound up in recounting His great deeds.

An account of David praising the name of the LORD in the closing days of his life is also found in 1 Chronicles 29. He specifically addresses the impending construction of the temple. David was not allowed by the LORD to construct the temple. But the LORD promised that David's son would build the temple. David has amassed the materials for the temple. His son Solomon will tend to the actual construction. Joyfully anticipating the construction of the temple after his death, David thinks upon all that the LORD has done to allow this time to arrive. He prays,

"Now we thank You, our God, and praise Your glorious name" (1 Chronicles 29:13). The pattern continues as God and His name are placed in parallel so that they cannot be separated. The other regular element, namely, that praise consists of recounting the deeds of the Lord, is also present.

As the prayer book of the Bible, the Psalms capture the biblical understanding of praise. Since David is the author of many psalms and we have already seen his concern for praising the name of the Lord, it is not surprising to find psalms that praise the name of the Lord. The twin themes of the inseparability of the Lord and His name and praise consisting of recounting the Lord's great deeds are consistently found in the Psalms. Here is a sampling of psalms that focus upon praising the name of the Lord.

- Psalm 7:17—"I will give to the Lord the thanks due to His righteousness, and I will sing praise to the name of the Lord, the Most High."
  David wrote this psalm as a plea for the Lord to deliver him from his pursuers. The psalm concludes with the natural result of the Lord's deliverance: namely, David praising the name of the Lord.

- Psalm 8:1—"O Lord, our Lord, how majestic is Your name in all the earth! You have set Your glory above the heavens."
  David wrote this psalm with a focus upon the majesty of the cosmos as created by the Lord. The beauty of His creation prompts the praise of the name of the Lord.

- Psalm 9:2—"I will be glad and exult in You; I will sing praise to Your name, O Most High."

David wrote this psalm as well. This verse immediately follows David's proclamation that he will recount the deeds of the LORD. The LORD's actions on David's behalf prompt David to praise His name.

- Psalm 18:49—"For this I will praise You, O LORD, among the nations, and sing to Your name." David begins this verse with "for," that is, "because of." Because of all the great deeds of salvation that David recounts in the first forty-eight verses of this psalm, praise of the name of the LORD pours forth.

- Psalm 44:8—"In God we have boasted continually, and we will give thanks to Your name forever." This psalm praises the name of the LORD despite many troubles that are described. Great troubles swirl about, but praise is still found because the psalmist knows what the LORD has done in the past.

- Psalm 66:1–2—"Shout for joy to God, all the earth; sing the glory of His name; give to Him glorious praise!" This psalm continues the pattern of praise being engendered by the actions of the LORD. The next verse of the psalm says to God, "How awesome are Your deeds." Verse 4 proclaims that the earth sings praises to the LORD and that the earth sings praises to His name, equating the LORD and His name.

- Psalm 99:3—"Let them praise Your great and awesome name! Holy is He!" This psalm rejoices in the LORD's justice and righteousness. It grounds those upon the Lord's actions on behalf of Moses and Aaron.

- Psalm 106:47—"Save us, O Lord our God, and gather us from among the nations, that we may give thanks to Your holy name and glory in Your praise." The cause of praise is the same as in the past. The Lord saves, and thus His people praise His name.

- Psalm 122:3–4—"Jerusalem—built as a city that is bound firmly together, to which the tribes go up, the tribes of the Lord, as was decreed for Israel, to give thanks to the name of the Lord."
  This is among David's Songs of Ascents. As the faithful ascended Zion to go to the temple, they would sing this song among others. The Lord's name is praised because of what the Lord does for His people in the temple.

- Psalm 142:7—"Bring me out of prison, that I may give thanks to Your name!"
  David wrote this psalm describing the time when he was in the cave, hiding from Saul. He calls upon the Lord to save him, which will then result in David's praise of the name of the Lord.

— Hallowed Be the Name of the Lord —

Not only is the name of the Lord to be praised, but His name is also to be hallowed. Jesus teaches the Church to pray "Hallowed be Thy name" as the First Petition of the Lord's Prayer. His name is holy in and of itself, but it is to be treated as the holy thing it is. Grammatically, *Hallowed* is passive, meaning that the subject receives the action of the verb. In English, we express the agent by which the passive verb is accomplished with a prepositional phrase beginning with "by." Yet Jesus does not give us the agent by whom God's name is hallowed. This is common in Scripture. When the agent is unexpressed, the passive verb is typically a so-called "theological passive" in that God is the agent by which the passive verb is accomplished. Who does the hallowing of God's name? The Lord hallows God's name Himself as He works in and through us.

This petition is also eschatological. While the Lord's name should be hallowed here and now, and while we pray that His name would be hallowed among us, honesty reveals that His name is not hallowed as it should be. We continue to pray for His name to be hallowed here and now with the confidence that the fulfillment of this petition will be realized on the Last Day. When Christ returns, then every tongue will confess Him, hallowing His name.

Luther grants helpful insight into this petition in the Large Catechism. In paragraph 38 of the First Petition, the Large Catechism teaches, "This name should have its proper honor; it should be valued holy and grand as the greatest treasure and holy thing that we have." The word translated as "holy thing" was the term used in Luther's day for a relic. At the time of the Reformation, relics received great attention. The faithful were told that if they adored a splinter from the cross of Christ, a bone from a saint, or some other relic, they would gain merit with God. Luther and the reformers taught clearly against the adoration of relics. Yet, here Luther gives focus to a true relic. The name of the Lord is a true holy thing.

> The Lord hallows God's name Himself as He works in and through us.

— Liturgical Delivery —
of the Name of the Lord

Scripture teaches us to call upon the name of the Lord, bless His holy name, give thanks to His name, praise His name, and hallow His name. In doing so, we worship Him because He and His name are inseparable. This worship focuses upon what He has done for us and upon His delivering the benefits of His work to us. The apostle John proclaims the benefit we receive from the name of the Lord: "These are written so that you may believe that Jesus is the Christ, the Son of God, and that by believing you may have life in His name" (John 20:31). Life is bound up in the name of Christ. The life of Christ, eternal life, victory over death, is given you in His name. The Church's liturgy, therefore, delivers His name so that you have life.

THE DIVINE SERVICE

Lutherans have historically used the term "Divine Service" to state why we gather. God serves us. He does not need what we bring to Him, though He delights to receive our praise and even more to receive our sin that we be forgiven. We direly need what He gives. So He serves us with His good gifts. Those gifts are given in His name. Within the Divine Service, the name of the Lord takes center stage, from Invocation to Benediction.

> The life of Christ, eternal life, victory over death, is given in His name.

The Divine Service begins with the Invocation: "In the name of the Father and of the Son and of the Holy Spirit." The first gift given by the Lord as He serves us is His triune name. It is a promise that we are served not by a generic god but by a very specific God who has revealed Himself to us by His name. The Invocation also recalls our Baptism into the name of God (Matthew 28:19). It is as if the Lord is saying to us, "I made you My own in Baptism, placing My name upon you and delivering to you all My goodness bound up in My name; now I give you My goodness anew."

The Divine Service closes with the Benediction: "The Lord bless you and keep you. The Lord make His face to shine upon you and be gracious unto you. The Lord lift up His countenance upon you and give you peace." These words were first given by the Lord Himself to Moses with the instruction that Aaron and his sons were to speak them over the Lord's people. Thus, this is often referred to as the Aaronic Benediction, as it was used by Aaron and his sons, who were the first priests. The Lord repeats His name throughout the Benediction, and He reveals what He gives in those words: "So they shall put My name upon the people of Israel, and I will bless them" (Numbers 6:27). In the Benediction, you receive the Lord's name anew. His name does not wear off from when you received it in Baptism. But you cannot receive His name too often. In the Benediction, it is as if the Lord says, "I gave you My name in Baptism. Now I give you My name anew so that you go forth in full confidence, knowing that I dwell with you."

The Divine Service is framed by the name of the Lord with the Invocation and the Benediction, highlighting the centrality of His name in the life of the Church. He continually delivers His name throughout the Divine Service.

His name is front and center in Confession and Absolution. Among the biblical passages often used within the liturgy of Confession and Absolution is "Our help is in the name of the Lord" (Psalm 124:8). It is a fitting text to find upon the lips of the faithful as they confess their sins because they know there is but one place to find the help they need, one place to find forgiveness: in the LORD who delivers forgiveness to us in His name. The Absolution is delivered by the LORD through the pastor with the words "Upon this your confession, I, by virtue of my office, as a called and ordained servant of the Word, announce the grace of God unto all of you, and in the stead and by the command of my Lord Jesus Christ I forgive you all your sins in the name of the Father and of the Son and of the Holy Spirit." With the authority of Christ given in John 20:19–23, the pastor forgives in the name of the LORD. As the words of the Absolution make clear, the faithful are not receiving the pastor's forgiveness. That is fine and good, but his forgiveness does not deliver the life of Christ. He is speaking by the authority of Christ, in the name of the LORD, delivering the LORD's forgiveness, which brings life.

While the pastoral office is holy, the man in the office remains a sinner. Having been absolved and cleansed of his sin, the pastor enters the chancel following Confession and Absolution, during the Introit. The Introit is typically a psalm chanted responsively by pastor and congregation. The psalm fits the theme of the day and puts the focus upon what the LORD has done, is doing, and promises to do for His people. (As we saw earlier in this chapter, this is the norm for psalms.) The Introit includes the Gloria Patri, where the faithful chant, "Glory be to the Father and to the Son and to the Holy Spirit; as it was in the beginning, is now, and will be forever." The triune name of the LORD comes center stage as He is praised for what He has done for His people.

Next within the Divine Service is the Kyrie. Like most liturgical terms, *Kyrie* is a transliteration of the first word of this liturgical element. *Kyrie* is Greek for "Lord!" The name of the LORD is in focus as the faithful cry out, "Lord, have mercy. Christ, have mercy. Lord, have mercy." Inspired by Mark 10:47 and borrowing language that is used regularly in the Psalms, the Kyrie turns the faithful to the Lord as their sole source of mercy and as the one who delivers mercy through His name.

The Collect of the Day follows as it collects the readings into a prayer that focuses upon the common thread uniting the service into a cohesive whole. The Collect is typically prayed to the Father "through Jesus Christ, Your Son, our Lord, who lives and reigns with You and the Holy Spirit, one God, now and forever." The triune name of God comes to the fore as the Collect is offered by faith in the name of the Lord.

The Creed (whether Apostles', Nicene, or Athanasian) focuses upon the triune name of God with reference to Father, Son, and Holy Spirit. The Creed gives attention to the Lord being known for what He does for our sake—creating, redeeming, and sanctifying us—much as the Psalms give attention to the name of the Lord being about His work for us.

The Prayer of the Church regularly changes from Sunday to Sunday to reflect the specific needs of the Church. There are consistent elements each week. Petitions for the Church throughout the world, for civil government, for the ill, for worthy reception of the Lord's Supper, and of thanks for the faithful who have gone before us are present each week. Setting Five of the Divine Service within the *Lutheran Service Book* orders the Prayer of the Church upon the Lord's Prayer. The First Petition includes these words: "Graciously turn from us all false doctrine and evil living whereby Your precious name is blasphemed and profaned." That is not the only instance when the name of the Lord comes into view. The Prayer of the Church is regularly prayed "through Jesus Christ, our Lord." Jesus promises that anything asked in His name will be done (John 14:14). With the Third Petition of the Lord's Prayer—"Thy will be done"—in mind, the faithful trust that when they pray in Jesus' name, they are submitting to

His wisdom rather than garnering His assent to their desires by simply speaking His name.

The Service of the Sacrament gives attention to the name of the LORD at various points. The triune name of the LORD is used within the Proper Preface, which reflects the season of the Church Year and yet recognizes that every season is the time of the Trinity's good gifts. The Sanctus uses the song of the seraphim from Isaiah 6 in recognition that in the Supper we are in the presence of the Holy LORD. To that song, the Sanctus adds the appellation spoken by the crowd on Palm Sunday: "Blessed is He who comes in the name of the Lord." The name of the LORD also comes into view with the Words of Institution. Setting Five of the Divine Service in *Lutheran Service Book* (based upon Luther's German Mass) introduces the Words of Institution by saying, "In the name of our Lord and Savior Jesus Christ, at His command, and with His own words, we receive His testament." Following reception of the Supper, the faithful pray a collect that is again offered in the triune name of the LORD. The Benediction then pulls together the rhythm of the name of the LORD from the Divine Service into glorious peace.

PRAYER OFFICES

The Church has been blessed with canonical hours of prayer that give rhythm to daily life. One of those prayer offices is Matins, which is prayed in the morning. The name of the LORD gives rhythm to Matins. As in the Introit of the Divine Service, the Gloria Patri gives voice to the faithful within Matins as we praise the LORD for His gifts to us. The Te Deum is the Church's historic hymn of praise within the order of Matins. The Te Deum includes, "O Lord, save Your people and bless Your heritage. Govern them and lift them up forever. Day by day we magnify

You, And we worship Your name forever and ever." We worship His name because the LORD cannot be separated from His name. While the Aaronic Benediction is delivered within the Divine Service, Matins blesses us with the Pauline Benediction, taken from 2 Corinthians 13:14. "The grace of our Lord Jesus Christ and the love of God and the communion of the Holy Spirit be with you all" brings the goodness of the name of the LORD through reference to the Trinity.

Vespers is the prayer office for the late afternoon. Like Matins, it extols and delivers the gifts bound up in the name of the LORD with the Gloria Patri and Pauline Benediction. Vespers also brings the LORD's name within the Responsory, which is chanted following the Scripture readings. The Responsory fills the ears of the faithful with Psalm 86:11: "Unite my heart to fear Your name that I may walk in Your truth." During the seasons of Advent and Lent, the Responsory changes to match the season. The Advent Responsory has the faithful rejoicing in the name of the LORD as we chant Jeremiah 23:6: "This is the name by which He will be called: The Lord Is Our Righteousness."

We worship His name because the LORD cannot be separated from His name.

Other prayer offices—Morning Prayer, Evening Prayer, and Compline (prayed at the close of the day)—do not neglect the name of the LORD. Through the Gloria Patri and the Pauline Benediction, the LORD continues to deliver the gifts bound up in His name.

Hymnody

The name of the Lord overflows in the hymnody of the Church as well. The following list with brief descriptions is far from exhaustive. This is enough to tickle your fancy so that your ears are attentive to the regularity with which the name of the Lord is found in hymnody, and so that you go looking for it.

"Holy, Holy, Holy" (*LSB* 507)—Stanza 4 of this well-known trinitarian hymn proclaims, "All Thy works shall praise Thy name in earth and sky and sea."

"At the Name of Jesus" (*LSB* 512)—This end-times hymn begins with reference to the teaching that on the Last Day every knee will bow at the name of Jesus (Philippians 2:10).

"All Hail the Power of Jesus' Name" (*LSB* 549)—The title of this well-known hymn confesses that the Lord and His authority are bound up in the name of Jesus.

"Before the Throne of God Above" (*LSB* 574)—A double blessing is found in this hymn. Stanza 2 confesses, "My name is graven on His hands, My name is written on His heart," which is drawn from Isaiah 49:15–16. There is blessing in your name being written there. Further blessing is found in stanza 1: "Before the throne of God above I have a strong, a perfect plea: A great High Priest, whose name is Love, Who ever lives and pleads for me." Since His name defines Him, there is joy that Christ, our High Priest, is defined by and named Love.

"My Hope Is Built on Nothing Less" (*LSB* 576)—
Confidence is found in this hymn as we sing, "My
hope is built on nothing less Than Jesus' blood and
righteousness; No merit of my own I claim But wholly
lean on Jesus' name."

"Thy Strong Word" (*LSB* 578)—Having confessed the
Lord's provision in the first four stanzas, stanza 5 asks
the Lord, "Give us lips to sing Thy glory, Tongues Thy
mercy to proclaim, Throats that shout the hope that
fills us, Mouths to speak Thy holy name." When the
Lord gives us such mouths, He is answering the First
Petition of the Lord's Prayer so that we live in accord
with the Second Commandment.

"Baptized into Your Name, Most Holy" (*LSB* 590)—
This baptismal hymn begins with the foundation of
Baptism, the name of the Lord given us in Baptism.
The rest of the hymn should be understood as extolling
all that is ours because we have received His name.

"I Bind unto Myself Today" (*LSB* 604)—St. Patrick's hymn
begins, "I bind unto myself today The strong name of
the Trinity." With His name come all His gifts, which
are then set forth throughout the rest of the hymn.

"For All the Saints" (*LSB* 677)—We give thanks to the
Lord for the saints who have gone before us, singing,
"For all the saints who from their labors rest, Who
Thee by faith before the world confessed, Thy name, O
Jesus, be forever blest." The name of Jesus and there-
fore Jesus Himself are due praise for having sanctified
and saved the saints.

"I Trust, O Lord, Your Holy Name" (*LSB* 734)—We sing our faith in the LORD's name because He has bound Himself to His name. Trusting in His name, the hymn then speaks of faith and confidence found in His Word, His strength, His faithfulness, and more.

"Forth in Thy Name, O Lord, I Go" (*LSB* 854)—As you go forth in the name of the LORD, you are acting on His behalf. This calls you both to fulfill your calling to your utmost ability and to rejoice that you are His hands for the sake of another.

"With the Lord Begin Your Task" (*LSB* 869)—This morning hymn calls us to engage in the tasks of the day with confidence that Christ attends us. The hymn concludes, "Jesus, in Your name begun Be the day's endeavor; Grant that it may well be done To Your praise forever." For the faithful, each day is the LORD's and thus is begun in His name.

"Jesus! Name of Wondrous Love" (*LSB* 900)—The eighth day of Christmas, January 1, is appointed for the celebration of the Circumcision and Naming of Jesus (Luke 2:21). When Jesus was circumcised in fulfillment of the Law, He was given His name. This hymn celebrates what is packed into the name of Jesus. The stanzas successively begin, "Jesus! Name of wondrous love," "Jesus! Name decreed of old," "Jesus! Name of priceless worth," "Jesus! Name of mercy mild," "Jesus! Only name that's giv'n," "Jesus! Name of wondrous love."

"Savior, Again to Thy Dear Name We Raise" (*LSB* 917)— As the faithful depart from the Divine Service, this

hymn has two overt references to the name of the
Lord. The hymn begins, "Savior, again to Thy dear
name we raise With one accord our parting hymn of
praise." The second stanza concludes, "Guard Thou
the lips from sin, the hearts from shame, That in this
house have called upon Thy name." Having worshiped
the Lord, the faithful pray that their lips and hearts
would honor His name.

"Holy God, We Praise Thy Name" (*LSB* 940)—This fourth-
century Latin hymn has stood the test of time. It is
a versification of the Te Deum. The Lord's name is
brought up immediately, and the rest of the hymn can
be rightly understood as unfolding what the Lord
gives in His name.

— Body and Mouth in One Accord —

This chapter has focused upon the name of the Lord in the
life of the Church, especially regarding how our mouths
confess His name in song and liturgy. The hymns have pointed
out that what the mouth says should be reflected in our actions
(for example, "Forth in Thy Name, O Lord, I Go"). As holistic
beings, that which our lips confess should be seen in our bodies.
One means by which this can be observed is in our bodily posture.

The rubrics (the italicized red instructions within *LSB*) direct
us to stand or kneel at various points of the service. While the
rubrics are not given by divine command, there is great wisdom
in them. What you do with your body will have an impact
upon the rest of you. Standing regularly communicates respect.
In a courtroom, you stand as the judge enters and leaves the

chambers. Gentlemen will stand when a lady enters the room. Even when (perhaps, especially when) you are not respectfully disposed, standing benefits you as it teaches you that you should be respectful despite your feelings. In the Divine Service, we stand for Invocation, Confession and Absolution, the Gospel, the Creed, Prayers, and the Service of the Sacrament.

Kneeling communicates humility. A young (or not-so-young) man drops to a knee when asking for a woman's hand in marriage. A sorrowful man does the same. There is wisdom in the hymnal's rubrics that direct us to kneel in humility for Confession and Absolution. It also makes sense that we drop to our knees at the table of the King of kings and Lord of lords as He feeds us with His body and blood.

And what about when the LORD's name is spoken? The rubrics do not give us direction, but we can learn well from Moses. On Mount Sinai, the LORD proclaims His name to Moses, revealing His very self. Moses responds by bowing his head to the earth and prostrating himself (Exodus 34:8). The name of the LORD delivers His presence; Moses knows the proper posture to take in the presence of the LORD. It serves us well to do the same. When the name of the LORD is given us in the Divine Service—Invocation, Absolution, Gloria Patri, Benediction—it is proper for us to bow the head in reverence, for the LORD is present.

Study Questions

1. "The joy of the Last Day is bound up in the name of the LORD." How is this true?

2. How does the *Carmen Christi* capture end-times joy in the name of the LORD?

3. What naturally results from Jesus revealing the name of the LORD?

4. Describe the parallelism of Psalm 96:2.

5. What is the focus of worship?

6. Why praise the name of the LORD?

7. Contrast acknowledging the name of the LORD as a true holy thing with the adoration of relics.

8. How is the name of the LORD found within the Divine Service?

9. What is your favorite hymn that extols the name of the LORD? Why?

10. Do you find it helpful to bow your head at the name of the LORD? Why or why not?

O MY GOD:
The Name of the
LORD in the Life
of the Christian

"Can you believe how she acted?"

"Yeah. Talk about over the top!"

"I know. I would be so embarrassed, but not her. She is oblivious to everyone else. Can you imagine what her family must be thinking?"

"I feel bad for them because they do understand how inappropriate she was. Did you see their faces?"

"OMG! I thought some of them were going to crawl under the seats to hide."

The vain use of "Oh my God" is so pervasive in our society that we even have an abbreviation for it. Think about the grammar of the phrase. "O my God" is used in Scripture as a vocative, a direct address. We call someone's name to get that person's attention, often so that we can ask for assistance. But when "OMG" fills our discourse, it is empty of that meaning. Instead of asking for God's help, the phrase substitutes for "I am shocked," draining the phrase of the weight that ought to come with reference to God.

Contrast that flippant usage with the vocative, direct address of God in Scriptures, such as in Psalm 130:1, 5, 7: "Out of the depths I cry to You, O Lord! . . . I wait for the Lord, my soul waits, and in His word I hope. . . . O Israel, hope in the Lord! For with the Lord there is steadfast love, and with Him is plentiful redemption!" With the psalmist, you can cry out, "O Lord!" with confidence, knowing that He hears you and gives answer to your need. He knows your need even before you ask. He provides even when you do not see the need. His provision matches your need rather than your desire. It flows from His character. As the psalmist says, "With the Lord there is steadfast love, and with Him there is plentiful redemption!" That is why you can hope in His Word. And that is why your faithful cry is "O Lord!" or "O my God!" Come to my aid.

This is the daily life of the Christian. A Christian is one who has received the name of the Lord that reveals His goodness and who calls upon Him with confidence. The rhythm of the Christian life is remembering His name, calling upon His name, receiving His goodness through His name, and then praising His name.

— Remembering the Name of the Lord —

The name of the Lord is to be remembered by His people. When He revealed His name to Moses on Mount Sinai, He instructed Moses to tell His people, "'The Lord, the God of your fathers, the God of Abraham, the God of Isaac, and the God of Jacob, has sent me to you.' This is My name forever, and thus I am to be remembered throughout all generations" (Exodus 3:15). Into His name, the Lord packs Himself, and through His name, He delivers the benefits of His work on behalf of His people. Remembering the name of the Lord through all generations (and specifically in your own generation and life) includes remembering all that He does with His name. Remembering the name of the Lord involves rejoicing in who He is. Remembering the name of the Lord includes faithful reception of His good gifts through His name. Remembering the name of the Lord means giving Him due thanks for those gifts in your daily life.

Remembering His name also calls you to remember the Lord's reputation. As the psalmist sings, "Your name, O Lord, endures forever, Your renown, O Lord, throughout all ages" (Psalm 135:13). His name and His renown (reputation) are two sides of the same coin. The Apostles' Creed serves as a good summary of His renown as Creator, Redeemer, and Sanctifier. That is among the reasons that the recitation of the Creed has been part of the daily rhythm of Christians through the ages. You also remember Him and His reputation in Confession and Absolution. The General Confession used within the Divine Service often includes the basis of forgiveness being "for the sake of the holy, innocent, bitter suffering and death of Your beloved Son." There is God's reputation. While we corporately engage in the General Confession in the Divine Service, the individual Christian life is blessed with Individual Confession and Absolution. The order for it is found on page 292 of *Lutheran Service Book* and is based upon the rite in Luther's Small Catechism. The Confession concludes, "I am sorry for all of this and ask for grace. I want to do better." I ask for grace. Why? Because the LORD is renowned for His grace and mercy. Individual Confession and Absolution, while not commanded by God, is given by the LORD as a means to receive the blessings packed into His name as you are forgiven in the name of the Father and of the Son and of the Holy Spirit. That is the Christian life. Luther puts it this way in "A Brief Exhortation to Confession," which he added to the Large Catechism: "When I urge you to go to Confession, I am doing nothing else than urging you to be a Christian" (*Concordia*, Appendix B, Brief Exhortation 32).

Remembering the name of the LORD also calls you to live by His Word. "I remember Your name in the night, O LORD, and keep Your law" (Psalm 119:55). The dynamics of Hebrew poetry are seen in this passage as the second half of the verse results from the first half. It could be translated causally: "I remember Your name in the night, O LORD, and *so* I keep Your law." While our ears are attuned to hearing the word *law* used specifically to refer to the righteous demands of God, in this verse "law" is used in a broader sense

> **The LORD is renowned for His grace and mercy.**

that encapsulates the whole of His teaching, both the Law that shows forth the LORD's demands and His Gospel that delivers the benefits of Christ to us. Remembering the name of the LORD, therefore, involves living by the Law and the Gospel. When I transgress the Law, I am not remembering (that is, I am not honoring) the name of the LORD. Yet when I trust in Christ for forgiveness as the Gospel promises, then His name is rightly remembered.

This is true at all times in life, both in prosperity and in adversity. Job is a prime example. When life was good, he remembered the name of the Lord so that he was pious and upright, fearing God and turning from evil (Job 1:1). He would offer sacrifices on behalf of his children (Job 1:5). Since Christ has fulfilled the sacrificial system by His own death, parents are no longer called upon to offer sacrifices for their children's sin. Yet parents still follow Job's example as they implore the Lord to guard, protect, bless, forgive, and keep their children in the faith. Job also remembered the name of the Lord in trials. When he loses all his children for whom he offered sacrifices, he responds by saying, "The Lord gave, and the Lord has taken away; blessed be the name of the Lord" (Job 1:21). The name of the Lord is not an amulet to ensure prosperity or a silver bullet to destroy all troubles. Those who remember His name are no more insulated from hardship than Job was. Yet, as they remember His name, they have strength to endure amid trial.

— Remembering Your Baptism —

You remember the name of the Lord when you remember your Baptism. In Baptism, you receive His name according to Christ's institution of Baptism in the name of the Father and of the Son and of the Holy Spirit. Bearing His name means that you are His. He has claimed you as His own. And if you are His, then He also is yours. There is no other god for you because the Lord has put His name upon you that He alone might be God for you. Gone are all idols. To put it simply, I am His; He is mine.

Paul delves into this dynamic in Romans 6. This passage is set up by what immediately precedes it: "Where sin increased, grace abounded all the more" (Romans 5:20). Paul knows what the sinful nature likes to do with this—twist and pervert it as an excuse to sin. "Hey, this is a great deal! The more I sin, the more grace I receive. So, let's keep on sinning." Paul responds in Romans 6:1–2: "What shall we say then? Are we to continue in sin that grace may abound? By no means! How can we who died to sin still live in it?" The grammar of Paul's phrase "by no means" is quite telling. It uses a verbal aspect called the optative that is quite rare in biblical Greek, which makes it jump off the page. The optative drives at the impossibility of something. When Paul says, "By no means," he is saying that it is not within the realm of possibility. It is unthinkable to use God's grace as an excuse for sin.

Why? Because you have died to sin. "How can we who died to sin still live in it?" When did you die? Paul continues, "Do you not know that all of us who have been baptized into Christ Jesus were baptized into His death?" (Romans 6:3). When the Lord put His name upon you in Baptism, among the blessings you received was that you died. Your sinful nature was drowned in Baptism. Paul does not say that Baptism represents, symbolizes, or points to death. He says death actually happened. In your Baptism, you died to sin. Christ's death became your own because He bound Himself to you in Baptism. All that is Christ's is now yours because you bear the name of the Lord.

It gets even better. When the Lord put His name upon you in Baptism, you also rose. "We were buried therefore with Him by baptism into death, in order that, just as Christ was raised from the dead by the glory of the Father, we too might walk in newness of life" (Romans 6:4). Again, Paul does not say that Baptism represents, symbolizes, or points to resurrection. He says it actually happened. In your Baptism, you were raised to life. Christ's resurrection became your own because He bound Himself to you in Baptism. When you have the name of the Lord, you have all His goodness.

This is why God's grace is never an excuse to sin. His grace is yours because you have been baptized in His name. You died to sin and you rose to new life, all because you have His name in Baptism. Yet the Christian life is not that easy. The sinful nature continues to rejoice in sin. In Romans 7, Paul talks about the battle within every Christian, the battle between your sinful nature and the new self that has risen from the baptismal waters. It is a battle. A key to winning that daily battle is to remember your Baptism.

> **All that is Christ's is now yours because you bear the name of the Lord.**

In this life, you will not be free of your sinful nature. But you have the perfect weapon against the sinful nature. You have the name of the Lord given you in Baptism. When temptation comes alluring, you can respond, "I am baptized. I am dead to sin; I have new life in Christ. Sin shall not master me." When temptation overpowers you and you are seduced by sin, you have the perfect response: "I am baptized. Sin does not own me; sin's name is not upon me. The name of the Lord is upon me. I am His, and He will not share me with sin. He forgives my sin that I may be His own."

Simply put, I am His; He is mine.

— Taking Refuge in the Name of the Lord —

Living out your Baptism in the name of the Lord includes the refuge you have in His name. This is a regular theme in the Psalms. It is found in Psalm 9:9–10: "The Lord is a stronghold for the oppressed, a stronghold in times of trouble. And those who know Your name put their trust in You, for You, O Lord, have not forsaken those who seek You." This is not a naïve belief that you will not have troubles. It is quite the opposite. In this psalm, David assures you that you will have troubles. But when oppressed, you have a refuge. You know the name given you in Baptism, so you have confidence in the face of oppression. His name is everlasting, so it remains with you from Baptism to eternity. That means He will not forsake you, because He does not quit on His name.

The refuge of His name is greater than where we often seek our confidence. David teaches us again, this time in Psalm 20:5, 7: "May we shout for joy over Your salvation, and in the name of our God set up our banners! May the LORD fulfill all your petitions! . . . Some trust in chariots and some in horses, but we trust in the name of the LORD our God." This is an incredible thing for David to say, since he is known as a great warrior. Chariots and horses are all about military might. We rightly pray for those who serve in the armed forces, asking the LORD to bless them and use them to keep at bay those who would do us harm. Yet military might will fail. And there are battles where chariots and horses cannot prevail. In the battle with sin, our banners are set up in the name of our God. He has won the victory. And He gives us the victory over sin by setting His name upon us.

The theme continues in Psalm 44, though this psalm was not written by David. "Through You we push down our foes; through Your name we tread down those who rise up against us" (v. 5). Lest this verse be hijacked and falsely seen as the means to ensure victory in the sports arena, politics, business, or whatever venue has grabbed your attention, remember that Scripture has a greater battle in mind. St. Paul instructs us, "For we do not wrestle against flesh and blood, but against the rulers, against the authorities, against the cosmic powers over this present darkness, against the spiritual forces of evil in the heavenly places" (Ephesians 6:12). Your strongest defense against the assaults of the devil is your

Baptism. You bear the name of the LORD. No matter how the evil foe should rage against you, he cannot undo what the LORD did for you in Baptism. Let him lodge accusations against you. You can reply, "I'm baptized in the name of the LORD."

David again teaches us in Psalm 124. This psalm is a Song of Ascents, which would have been sung as the faithful ascended Mount Zion as they headed to the temple for sacrifices—that is, for forgiveness. The entire psalm attests to the doom that the people would have faced if the LORD had not saved them. That theme builds until the final verse, where David teaches us to say, "Our help is in the name of the LORD, who made heaven and earth" (v. 8). This verse is found within the liturgy of Confession and Absolution. What is the chief help we find in the name of the LORD? Forgiveness of sin, by which we are freed from condemnation and granted eternal life. And where did you receive the name of the LORD, which grants you forgiveness, frees you from condemnation, and gives you eternal life? In your Baptism.

> "I'm baptized in the name of the LORD."

The Psalms are not alone in proclaiming the refuge and strength that is ours in the name of the LORD. Proverbs 18:10 joins in, saying, "The name of the LORD is a strong tower; the righteous man runs into it and is safe." The surrounding verses offer a contrast with riches and pride. Riches and self-confidence are not a strong tower. The name of the LORD is where you are kept safe. His name certainly grants safety eternally by means of Baptism. There is also temporal safety as His name offers perspective about what matters. When convinced that riches will grant you safety, you are ripe for destruction. When you trust in yourself so that pride takes hold, a great fall looms before you. These will fail you; the name of the LORD does not.

— Honoring the Name of the Lord —

Having received so much in the name of the Lord, we are called to honor His name. The name of the Lord is our greatest treasure because He has packed Himself into His name. It is fitting that we honor this treasure. Paul instructs us, "Whatever you do, in word or deed, do everything in the name of the Lord Jesus, giving thanks to God the Father through Him" (Colossians 3:17). Paul gives this as part of his exhortation to Christian living as we serve one another. Since you bear the name of the Lord, Christ is at work through you for the benefit of others. There is no distinction between sacred and secular actions for those who bear the name of the Lord. Every calling you have been given by the Lord is a sacred calling for the benefit of your neighbor. Thus, you are called to live out your callings to your utmost ability. The pastor who studies diligently in crafting a sermon honors the name of the Lord. The craftsman who applies his carpentry skills with keen attention to detail honors the name of the Lord. The doctor who gives heed to her patients' needs with care and precision honors the name of the Lord. On the other hand, the worker who is lackadaisical, even sloppy in his work, dishonors the name of the Lord.

Paul also teaches that our conduct is a testimony to others. "Let all who are under a yoke as slaves regard their own masters as worthy of all honor, so that the name of God and the teaching may not be reviled" (1 Timothy 6:1). This text should not be construed as justification for slavery. The ancient practice of slavery was rampant with abuse. The United States bears great shame from our own history of slavery. The prevalence of slavery today in the form of human trafficking should not be tolerated. Christians have historically been at the vanguard of abolitionism, and rightly so. What Paul is teaching Timothy and you is that your conduct toward those in authority over you will prompt them to either honor or revile the name of God. There is a proper time and means to speak against those in authority who are not using their authority to the holy ends that God intends. Yet when you speak against such abuse of authority and when you respond in general to the one in authority, you should do so in a manner that does not prompt them to revile the name of God.

> The name of the LORD is our greatest treasure. . . . It is fitting that we honor this treasure.

Even when you are faithful to honor the name of the LORD in your conduct toward others, there will be those who insult you because you bear the name of the LORD. Jesus says that people will speak evil against you falsely on His account. And He says that when it happens, you are blessed (Matthew 5:11). Having learned this from Christ in the Sermon on the Mount, Peter says, "If you are insulted for the name of Christ, you are blessed, because the Spirit of glory and of God rests upon you" (1 Peter 4:14). You are blessed when you are insulted for Christ's name because you are being formed into His image. In Baptism, He began to conform you to His image. It will come to completion on the day that Christ returns for us. Until then, Jesus is at work to transform you into His image. One of the chief ways is by having you suffer as He suffered. Even more, when you suffer for His name's sake, you are being molded in His image.

Marriage is also a setting in which the name of the LORD is to be honored. The Rite of Marriage is framed by the name of the LORD. It begins with the Invocation—in the name of the Father and of the Son and of the Holy Spirit. It concludes with the Benediction, which the Lord has established as a means by which His name is placed upon His people (Numbers 6:27).

There is plenty between Invocation and Benediction that reveals the weight of names. The Declaration of Intent uses the names of the couple—"I, Kevin, take you, Joy . . ." By their names, they are binding their very selves to each other. The Exchange of Rings is accompanied by each saying, "Receive this ring as a pledge and token of wedded love and faithfulness in the name of the Father and of the Son and of the Holy Spirit." In so doing, they acknowledge that while they are willing participants, it is the Lord Himself who is binding them together by the authority of His name. If the Exchange of Rings did not make this clear, the Proclamation of Marriage leaves no doubt. The pastor uses the names of the couple as well as the name of the Lord. "Now that Kevin and Joy have committed themselves to each other in holy matrimony, have given themselves to each other by their solemn pledges, and have declared the same before God and these witnesses, I pronounce them to be husband and wife, in the name of the Father and of the Son and of the Holy Spirit."

The names of husband and wife are bound together in the name of the Lord. The name of the Lord is honored when husband and wife, the Church, and all uphold marriage according to the purposes for which it was created by the Lord. Marriage is solemnized in His name because it is His estate. He created it; He crafted it with a proper order; He blesses it. Marriage is not for husband and wife (or anyone else) to do with as they please. To do so would be to dishonor the name of the Lord.

— The Name of the Lord in — Eschatological Perspective

The name of the Lord bears weight not only now but into eternity. The Revelation to St. John returns time and again to speak about the name of the Lord in the scope of eternity. In Revelation 11, the seventh trumpet is sounded, signaling the end of time. John writes, "The nations raged, but Your wrath came, and the time for the dead to be judged, and for rewarding Your servants, the prophets and saints, and those who fear Your name, both small and great, and for destroying the destroyers of the earth" (v. 18). The judgment separates those who are to be rewarded from those to be destroyed. The list of those who are rewarded is a group marked by their faithfulness, including the servants of the Lord, the prophets, the saints, and those who fear the name of the Lord. The last can be understood as a summation of the list. The servants, prophets, and saints are those who fear the name of the Lord and thus are rewarded with eternal life. This is not to be understood as saying that reverent fear earns entrance into eternal life. This is about faith in the name of the Lord, knowing that outside of His name, His authority, His very self, there would be no right to eternal life. This is comparable to worthy reception of the Lord's Supper. You are not worthy because you have fulfilled various requirements. You are worthy when you look outside yourself, away from your own sin, and find your worthiness in Christ and the forgiveness He delivers with His body and blood under bread and wine. So it is with fearing the name of the Lord. Such fear looks outside the self to Christ in whom there is worthiness to enter eternal life.

The forces of evil are also known for the names they bear. In Revelation 13, John describes tyrannical political power as one of the tools employed by the devil against the Church: "I saw a beast rising out of the sea, with ten horns and seven heads, with ten diadems on its horns and blasphemous names on its heads" (v. 1). When John wrote this, the Roman emperor was demanding that titles such as "lord," "divine," and "god" be given to him.

> **Those who fear the name of the LORD . . . are rewarded with eternal life.**

These would be the blasphemous names on the beast of tyrannical power. That sort of power remains present to this day and will remain until Christ returns as those in power seek to legitimize their power by claiming divine right to it.

John records a similar description later. He writes, "He carried me away in the Spirit into a wilderness, and I saw a woman sitting on a scarlet beast that was full of blasphemous names, and it had seven heads and ten horns. . . . And on her forehead was written a name of mystery: 'Babylon the great, mother of prostitutes and of earth's abominations'" (Revelation 17:3, 5). As Babylon had been the tyrannical power that had oppressed God's people in the sixth century BC, this passage describes Rome as the tyrannical power of John's day. The woman described in the passage has a name written on her forehead to mark her as belonging to Rome. This reveals her allegiance to Rome rather than to God.

A stark contrast is given in what is revealed to John about the faithful. In the letter to the Church in Philadelphia, Christ says, "The one who conquers, I will make him a pillar in the temple of My God. Never shall he go out of it, and I will write on him the name of My God, and the name of the city of My God, the new Jerusalem, which comes down from My God out of heaven, and My own new name" (Revelation 3:12). Christ promises to write the name of God, the name of the New Jerusalem (our eternal dwelling), and His own name upon His people. There is no doubt to whom they belong. They do not belong to Rome but to the New Jerusalem. They do not belong to a tyrant but to God and Christ.

This glorious revelation is given again in Revelation 14. John is granted a revelation of heaven, where he sees the faithful who are numbered as 144,000. The number 1,000 is a number used throughout Scripture but especially in Revelation to denote fullness and completion. The number 144 is 12 × 12. The number 12 is regularly used for the people of God, such as with 12 tribes of Israel and 12 disciples. Thus, 144,000 is Revelation's way of indicating the full number of God's people. Here is what is revealed of them to John: "Then I looked, and behold, on Mount Zion stood the Lamb, and with Him 144,000 who had His name and His Father's name written on their foreheads" (v. 1). They stand with the Lamb, Christ, who died and rose. And they have His name and the Father's name on their foreheads. There is no doubting to whom they belong.

The letter to Philadelphia gives a promise of what will be true for those still laboring on earth. Revelation 14:1 describes what is true for those now in heaven. Revelation 22:4 reveals what is true of the people of God in eternity: "They will see His face, and His name will be on their foreheads." When Christ comes again, you will see Him face-to-face, and you will bear His name.

In this life, in heaven, and in eternal life, you bear the name of the LORD. It is an eternal name that you cannot lose. There is no doubt to whom you belong because He has placed His name upon you. With His name comes His very self and all His benefits. He dwells with you. And where did you get that name? In Baptism.

— Morning and Evening Prayer —

All the blessings of the name of the LORD come to you in Baptism. It is fitting that you remember it daily. This is among the blessings of the Morning Prayer and Evening Prayer within Luther's Small Catechism. They follow a similar order. In the morning, when you get up, and in the evening, when you go to bed, make the sign of the holy cross and say, "In the name of the Father and of the Son and of the Holy Spirit." Your day is begun and ended in the name of the LORD. The same name that was placed upon you in Baptism carries you through each day. His grace attends you through whatever each day holds. The world seeks to lay claim to you, but the world cannot because you bear the name of another. You bear the name above all names so that when you bring your requests to God, they come with His authority. You suffer the disdain of the world, but you hold your head high because the name you bear has the highest renown. You face loneliness, yet you are never alone because His name delivers His very presence. You are discarded by others, but you are claimed by the One who put His name on you.

It is for good reason that you begin and end your day by remembering your Baptism into His name. The sign of the cross teaches you again that the benefits of the cross of Christ were given you with the name of the LORD. The Small Catechism then instructs you to repeat the Apostles' Creed and the Lord's Prayer. The Creed ever sets before you what is bound up in the name of the LORD, everything that He has done for you. The Lord's Prayer then sets into your mouth all that you need,

> The same name that was placed upon you in Baptism carries you through each day.

including the First Petition, where Jesus teaches you to ask: "Hallowed be Thy name." Then the Morning and Evening Prayers both commend you into the hands of the One who has set His name upon you.

With the day begun in the name and all the name delivers to you, you can go joyfully to the tasks of the day. With the day concluded in the name and all the name delivers to you, you can go to sleep in good cheer. You bear the name of the LORD. Your life is lived in the same confidence that David has: "He leads me in paths of righteousness for His name's sake" (Psalm 23:3).

Study Questions

1. Contrast "OMG" with Psalm 130.

2. Why is daily recitation of the Apostles' Creed a helpful way to remember the name of the LORD?

3. How does remembering the name of the LORD lead you to live by Law and Gospel?

4. How does Romans 6 answer the sinful nature's desire to keep to sinning? (Be sure to include baptismal death and resurrection in your answer.)

5. How is the name of the LORD a refuge for you?

6. You honor the name of the LORD by doing your utmost in all your callings. In what callings are you tempted to not do your utmost?

7. "In this life, in heaven, and in eternal life, you bear the name of the LORD." How is your baptismal identity enduring?

8. Spend a week faithfully praying both the Morning and the Evening Prayer daily. How did that discipline impact your life?

AFTERWORD

Often the most poignant theological reflections come from artists, including poets. With depth that begs for contemplation and richness that consistently satisfies, poetry delivers a glimpse at the beauty of God that transcends comprehension. The wealth that God packs into His name is glimpsed in the poetry of Jaroslav Vajda's hymn "In the Streets, in Home and Workplace."[7] The poem's meter matches that of the hymn tune *Irby*, best known for accompanying "Once in Royal David's City." Vajda describes the inspiration for this piece:

> For years, and increasingly of late, I have been distressed by the profanation of God's name in nearly every area of life and every segment of society, including the youngest of children. Can any person or society be blessed that treats the holiest name so frivolously? Can a God whose name (i.e., person) is so glibly and disrespectfully used be reverenced and loved as He deserves? Has God rescinded the commandment that holds anyone guilty who takes that holiest of names in vain?
>
> To protect that holy name, God's chosen people of the Old Testament did not utter the Tetragrammaton, the four letters YHVH, lest they take it in vain. Our use of anyone's name bespeaks our attitude toward that

7   Jaroslav J. Vajda, *Sing Peace, Sing Gift of Peace: The Comprehensive Hymnary of Jaroslav J. Vajda*, St. Louis: Concordia Publishing House, 2003, 136–37.

individual's personhood and identity. Next to ingratitude, the daily, universal abuse and blasphemy of God's name reveals one's stance toward the only Being whose grace alone can change our curses into blessings, beginning with the Creator and then proceeding to those created in His image.

I knew a reverent Christian who bowed his head every time he heard or said the name of Jesus. Suppose every grateful creature would even now bow the knee at the name of Jesus, as every creature in heaven and on earth will one day do? Must the Lord wait until then to be recognized and revered as He deserves?

My reflections mirror Vajda's. He captures the dissonance between what the Lord packs into His name and the common treatment of His name, the disparity between what is holy and yet is treated as common. As helpful as his prose description is, his poetic hymn text is even more compelling. He turns a phrase winsomely, calling upon us to treat the name of the Lord, YaHWeH, as "our choice four-letter word" since it appears as a four-consonant word when written in Hebrew. He works a great and powerful reversal as he takes three common phrases that diminish the name of the Lord and places them in their proper usage that honors His name as holy.

In the streets, in home and workplace,
everywhere Your Name is said,
turn the thoughtless, flippant phrases
into earnest praise instead.
YaHWeH, true, most holy Lord,
be our choice four-letter Word!

O my God, I die without you,
O my God, see my despair!
O my God, how much You love me!
O my God, how great You are!
Move me, help me to reclaim
Your most holy, precious Name!

Jesus Christ, the world's Redeemer!
Jesus Christ, God's only Son!
Jesus Christ, my Intercessor!
Jesus Christ, the Judge to come!
Move me, help me to acclaim
Your most holy saving Name!

For Christ's sake, have mercy on me!
For Christ's sake, forgive my sin!
For Christ's sake, bring peace among us!
For Christ's sake, new life begin!
Move me, help me to proclaim
Yours the only saving Name!